FOREWORD

The collection of "Everything Will Be Okay" travel phrasebooks published by T&P Books is designed for people traveling abroad for tourism and business. The phrasebooks contain what matters most - the essentials for basic communication. This is an indispensable set of phrases to "survive" while abroad.

This phrasebook will help you in most cases where you need to ask something, get directions, find out how much something costs, etc. It can also resolve difficult communication situations where gestures just won't help.

This book contains a lot of phrases that have been grouped according to the most relevant topics. A separate section of the book also provides a small dictionary with more than 1,500 important and useful words.

Take "Everything Will Be Okay" phrasebook with you on the road and you'll have an irreplaceable traveling companion who will help you find your way out of any situation and teach you to not fear speaking with foreigners.

TABLE OF CONTENTS

T&P Books Publishing

T&P Books Publishing

PHRASEBOOK
- JAPANESE -

THE MOST IMPORTANT PHRASES

This phrasebook contains
the most important
phrases and questions
for basic communication
Everything you need
to survive overseas

T&P BOOKS

By Andrey Taranov

Phrasebook + 1500-word dictionary

English-Japanese phrasebook & concise dictionary

By Andrey Taranov

The collection of "Everything Will Be Okay" travel phrasebooks published by T&P Books is designed for people traveling abroad for tourism and business. The phrasebooks contain what matters most - the essentials for basic communication. This is an indispensable set of phrases to "survive" while abroad.

Another section of the book also provides a small dictionary with more than 1,500 useful words arranged alphabetically. The dictionary includes a lot of gastronomic terms and will be helpful when ordering food at a restaurant or buying groceries at the store.

T&P Books Publishing
www.tpbooks.com

ISBN: 978-1-78492-435-5

This book is also available in E-book formats.
Please visit www.tpbooks.com or the major online bookstores.

PRONUNCIATION

Hiragana	Katakana	Rōmaji	Japanese example	T&P phonetic alphabet	English example

Consonants

Hiragana	Katakana	Rōmaji	Japanese example	T&P phonetic alphabet	English example
あ	ア	a	あなた	[a]	shorter than in ask
い	イ	i	いす	[i], [iː]	feet, Peter
う	ウ	u	うた	[u], [uː]	book, shoe
え	エ	e	いいえ	[e]	elm, medal
お	オ	o	しお	[ɔ]	bottle, doctor
や	ヤ	ya	やすみ	[jɑ]	young, yard
ゆ	ユ	yu	ふゆ	[ju]	youth, usually
よ	ヨ	yo	ようす	[jɔ]	New York

Syllables

Hiragana	Katakana	Rōmaji	Japanese example	T&P phonetic alphabet	English example
ば	バ	b	ばん	[b]	baby, book
ち	チ	ch	ちち	[ʧ]	cheese
だ	ダ	d	からだ	[d]	day, doctor
ふ	フ	f	ひふ	[f]	face, food
が	ガ	g	がっこう	[g]	game, gold
は	ハ	h	はは	[h]	home, have
じ	ジ	j	じしょ	[ʤ]	joke, general
か	カ	k	かぎ	[k]	clock, kiss
む	ム	m	さむらい	[m]	magic, milk
に	ニ	n	にもつ	[n]	name, normal
ぱ	パ	p	パン	[p]	pencil, private
ら	ラ	r	いくら	[r]	rice, radio
さ	サ	s	あさ	[s]	city, boss
し	シ	sh	わたし	[ɕ]	sheep, shop
た	タ	t	ふた	[t]	tourist, trip
つ	ツ	ts	いくつ	[ʦ]	cats, tsetse fly
わ	ワ	w	わた	[w]	vase, winter
ざ	ザ	z	ざっし	[ʣ]	beads, kids

LIST OF ABBREVIATIONS

English abbreviations

ab.	-	about
adj	-	adjective
adv	-	adverb
anim.	-	animate
as adj	-	attributive noun used as adjective
e.g.	-	for example
etc.	-	et cetera
fam.	-	familiar
fem.	-	feminine
form.	-	formal
inanim.	-	inanimate
masc.	-	masculine
math	-	mathematics
mil.	-	military
n	-	noun
pl	-	plural
pron.	-	pronoun
sb	-	somebody
sing.	-	singular
sth	-	something
v aux	-	auxiliary verb
vi	-	intransitive verb
vi, vt	-	intransitive, transitive verb
vt	-	transitive verb

JAPANESE PHRASEBOOK

This section contains
important phrases that may
come in handy in various
real-life situations.
The phrasebook will help
you ask for directions, clarify
a price, buy tickets, and
order food at a restaurant

T&P Books Publishing

PHRASEBOOK
CONTENTS

T&P Books Publishing

The bare minimum

Excuse me, ...	すみません、… [sumimasen, ...]
Hello.	こんにちは。 [konnichiwa]
Thank you.	ありがとうございます。 [arigatō gozai masu]
Good bye.	さようなら。 [sayōnara]
Yes.	はい。 [hai]
No.	いいえ。 [īe]
I don't know.	わかりません。 [wakari masen]
Where? | Where to? | When?	どこ？ | どこへ？ | いつ？ [doko ? | doko e ? | i tsu ?]

I need ...	…が必要です [... ga hitsuyō desu]
I want ...	したいです [shi tai desu]
Do you have ...?	…をお持ちですか？ [... wo o mochi desu ka ?]
Is there a ... here?	ここには…がありますか？ [koko ni wa ... ga ari masu ka ?]
May I ...?	…してもいいですか？ [... shi te mo ī desu ka ?]
..., please (polite request)	お願いします。 [onegai shi masu]

I'm looking for ...	…を探しています [... wo sagashi te i masu]
restroom	トイレ [toire]
ATM	ＡＴＭ [ētīemu]
pharmacy (drugstore)	薬局 [yakkyoku]
hospital	病院 [byōin]
police station	警察 [keisatsu]
subway	地下鉄 [chikatetsu]

taxi	タクシー [takushī]
train station	駅 [eki]

My name is ...	私は…と申します [watashi wa ... to mōshi masu]
What's your name?	お名前は何ですか？ [o namae wa nan desu ka ?]
Could you please help me?	助けていただけますか？ [tasuke te itadake masu ka ?]
I've got a problem.	困ったことがあります。 [komatta koto ga arimasu]
I don't feel well.	気分が悪いのです。 [kibun ga warui nodesu]
Call an ambulance!	救急車を呼んで下さい！ [kyūkyū sha wo yon de kudasai !]
May I make a call?	電話をしてもいいですか？ [denwa wo shi te mo ī desu ka ?]

I'm sorry.	ごめんなさい。 [gomennasai]
You're welcome.	どういたしまして。 [dōitashimashite]

I, me	私 [watashi]
you (inform.)	君 [kimi]
he	彼 [kare]
she	彼女 [kanojo]
they (masc.)	彼ら [karera]
they (fem.)	彼女たち [kanojotachi]
we	私たち [watashi tachi]
you (pl)	君たち [kimi tachi]
you (sg, form.)	あなた [anata]

ENTRANCE	入り口 [iriguchi]
EXIT	出口 [deguchi]
OUT OF ORDER	故障中 [koshō chū]
CLOSED	休業中 [kyūgyō chū]

OPEN

営業中
[eigyō chū]

FOR WOMEN

女性用
[josei yō]

FOR MEN

男性用
[dansei yō]

Questions

Where?
どこ？
[doko ?]

Where to?
どこへ？
[doko e ?]

Where from?
どこから？
[doko kara ?]

Why?
どうしてですか？
[dōshite desu ka ?]

For what reason?
なんのためですか？
[nan no tame desu ka ?]

When?
いつですか？
[i tsu desu ka ?]

How long?
どのぐらいですか？
[dono gurai desu ka ?]

At what time?
何時にですか？
[nan ji ni desu ka ?]

How much?
いくらですか？
[ikura desu ka ?]

Do you have ...?
…をお持ちですか？
[… wo o mochi desu ka ?]

Where is ...?
…はどこですか？
[… wa doko desu ka ?]

What time is it?
何時ですか？
[nan ji desu ka ?]

May I make a call?
電話をしてもいいですか？
[denwa wo shi te mo ī desu ka ?]

Who's there?
誰ですか？
[dare desu ka ?]

Can I smoke here?
ここでタバコを吸ってもいいですか？
[koko de tabako wo sutte mo ī desu ka ?]

May I ...?
…してもいいですか？
[… shi te mo ī desu ka ?]

Needs

I'd like …

…をしたいのですが
[… wo shi tai no desu ga]

I don't want …

…したくないです
[… shi taku nai desu]

I'm thirsty.

喉が渇きました。
[nodo ga kawaki mashi ta]

I want to sleep.

眠りたいです。
[nemuri tai desu]

I want …

したいです
[shi tai desu]

to wash up

洗いたい
[arai tai]

to brush my teeth

歯を磨きたい
[ha wo migaki tai]

to rest a while

しばらく休みたい
[shibaraku yasumi tai]

to change my clothes

着替えたい
[kigae tai]

to go back to the hotel

ホテルに戻る
[hoteru ni modoru]

to buy …

…を買う
[… wo kau]

to go to …

…へ行く
[… e iku]

to visit …

…を訪問する
[… wo hōmon suru]

to meet with …

…と会う
[… to au]

to make a call

電話をする
[denwa wo suru]

I'm tired.

疲れています。
[tsukare te i masu]

We are tired.

私たちは疲れました。
[watashi tachi wa tsukare mashita]

I'm cold.

寒いです。
[samui desu]

I'm hot.

暑いです。
[atsui desu]

I'm OK.

大丈夫です。
[daijōbu desu]

I need to make a call.　　　　　電話をしなければなりません。
　　　　　　　　　　　　　　　[denwa wo shi nakere ba nari masen]

I need to go to the restroom.　　トイレへ行きたいです。
　　　　　　　　　　　　　　　[toire e iki tai desu]

I have to go.　　　　　　　　　行かなければいけません。
　　　　　　　　　　　　　　　[ika nakere ba ike masen]

I have to go now.　　　　　　　今すぐ行かなければいけません。
　　　　　　　　　　　　　　　[ima sugu ika nakere ba ike masen]

Asking for directions

Excuse me, ...	すみません、… [sumimasen, ...]
Where is ...?	…はどこですか？ [... wa doko desu ka ?]
Which way is ...?	…はどちらですか？ [...wa dochira desu ka ?]
Could you help me, please?	助けていただけますか？ [tasuke te itadake masu ka ?]
I'm looking for ...	…を探しています [... wo sagashi te i masu]
I'm looking for the exit.	出口を探しています。 [deguchi wo sagashi te i masu]
I'm going to ...	…へ行く予定です [... e iku yotei desu]
Am I going the right way to ...?	…へはこの道で合っていますか？ [...e wa kono michi de atte i masu ka ?]
Is it far?	遠いですか？ [tōi desu ka ?]
Can I get there on foot?	そこまで歩いて行けますか？ [soko made arui te ike masu ka ?]
Can you show me on the map?	地図で教えて頂けますか？ [chizu de oshie te itadake masu ka ?]
Show me where we are right now.	今どこにいるかを教えて下さい。 [ima doko ni iru ka wo oshie te kudasai]
Here	ここです [koko desu]
There	あちらです [achira desu]
This way	こちらです [kochira desu]
Turn right.	右に曲がって下さい。 [migi ni magatte kudasai]
Turn left.	左に曲がって下さい。 [hidari ni magatte kudasai]
first (second, third) turn	1つ目（2つ目、3つ目） の曲がり角 [hitotsume (futatsume, mittsume) no magarikado]
to the right	右に [migi ni]

to the left   左に
[hidari ni]

Go straight.   まっすぐ歩いて下さい。
[massugu arui te kudasai]

Signs

WELCOME!	いらっしゃいませ！ [irasshai mase !]
ENTRANCE	入り口 [iriguchi]
EXIT	出口 [deguchi]
PUSH	押す [osu]
PULL	引く [hiku]
OPEN	営業中 [eigyō chū]
CLOSED	休業中 [kyūgyō chū]
FOR WOMEN	女性用 [josei yō]
FOR MEN	男性用 [dansei yō]
MEN, GENTS	男性用 [dansei yō]
WOMEN, LADIES	女性用 [josei yō]
DISCOUNTS	営業 [eigyō]
SALE	セール [sēru]
FREE	無料 [muryō]
NEW!	新商品！ [shin shōhin !]
ATTENTION!	目玉品！ [medama hin !]
NO VACANCIES	満員 [man in]
RESERVED	ご予約済み [go yoyaku zumi]
ADMINISTRATION	管理 [kanri]
STAFF ONLY	社員専用 [shain senyō]

BEWARE OF THE DOG! 猛犬注意
[mōken chūi]

NO SMOKING! 禁煙！
[kin en !]

DO NOT TOUCH! 触るな危険！
[sawaru na kiken !]

DANGEROUS 危ない
[abunai]

DANGER 危険
[kiken]

HIGH VOLTAGE 高電圧
[kō denatsu]

NO SWIMMING! 水泳禁止！
[suiei kinshi !]

OUT OF ORDER 故障中
[koshō chū]

FLAMMABLE 火気注意
[kaki chūi]

FORBIDDEN 禁止
[kinshi]

NO TRESPASSING! 通り抜け禁止！
[tōrinuke kinshi !]

WET PAINT ペンキ塗り立て
[penki nuritate]

CLOSED FOR RENOVATIONS 改装閉鎖中
[kaisō heisa chū]

WORKS AHEAD この先工事中
[kono saki kōji chū]

DETOUR 迂回
[ukai]

Transportation. General phrases

plane	飛行機
	[hikōki]
train	電車
	[densha]
bus	バス
	[basu]
ferry	フェリー
	[ferī]
taxi	タクシー
	[takushī]
car	車
	[kuruma]

schedule	時刻表
	[jikoku hyō]
Where can I see the schedule?	どこで時刻表を見られますか？
	[doko de jikoku hyō wo mirare masu ka ?]
workdays (weekdays)	平日
	[heijitsu]
weekends	週末
	[shūmatsu]
holidays	祝日
	[kokumin no syukujitsu]

DEPARTURE	出発
	[shuppatsu]
ARRIVAL	到着
	[tōchaku]
DELAYED	遅延
	[chien]
CANCELED	欠航
	[kekkō]

next (train, etc.)	次の
	[tsugi no]
first	最初の
	[saisho no]
last	最後の
	[saigono]

When is the next ...?	次の…はいつですか？
	[tsugi no ... wa i tsu desu ka ?]
When is the first ...?	最初の…はいつですか？
	[saisho no ... wa i tsu desu ka ?]

When is the last ...?

最後の…はいつですか？
[saigo no ... wa i tsu desu ka ?]

transfer (change of trains, etc.)

乗り継ぎ
[noritsugi]

to make a transfer

乗り継ぎをする
[noritsugi wo suru]

Do I need to make a transfer?

乗り継ぎをする必要がありますか？
[noritsugi o suru hitsuyō ga ari masu ka ?]

Buying tickets

Where can I buy tickets?	どこで乗車券を買えますか？ [doko de jōsha ken wo kae masu ka ?]
ticket	乗車券 [jōsha ken]
to buy a ticket	乗車券を買う [jōsha ken wo kau]
ticket price	乗車券の値段 [jōsha ken no nedan]
Where to?	どこへ？ [doko e ?]
To what station?	どこの駅へ？ [doko no eki e ?]
I need ...	…が必要です [... ga hitsuyō desu]
one ticket	券　1枚 [ken ichi mai]
two tickets	2枚 [ni mai]
three tickets	3枚 [san mai]
one-way	片道 [katamichi]
round-trip	往復 [ōfuku]
first class	ファーストクラス [fāsuto kurasu]
second class	エコノミークラス [ekonomī kurasu]
today	今日 [kyō]
tomorrow	明日 [ashita]
the day after tomorrow	あさって [asatte]
in the morning	朝に [asa ni]
in the afternoon	昼に [hiru ni]
in the evening	晩に [ban ni]

aisle seat

通路側の席
[tsūro gawa no seki]

window seat

窓側の席
[madogawa no seki]

How much?

いくらですか？
[ikura desu ka ?]

Can I pay by credit card?

カードで支払いができますか？
[kādo de shiharai ga deki masu ka ?]

Bus

bus	バス [basu]
intercity bus	高速バス [kōsoku basu]
bus stop	バス停 [basutei]
Where's the nearest bus stop?	最寄りのバス停はどこですか？ [moyori no basutei wa doko desu ka ?]
number (bus ~, etc.)	数 [kazu]
Which bus do I take to get to …?	…に行くにはどのバスに乗れば いいですか ？ […ni iku niwa dono basu ni nore ba ī desu ka …?]
Does this bus go to …?	このバスは…まで行きますか？ [kono basu wa … made iki masu ka ?]
How frequent are the buses?	バスはどのくらいの頻度で 来ますか？ [basu wa dono kurai no hindo de ki masu ka?]
every 15 minutes	１５分おき [jyū go fun oki]
every half hour	３０分おき [sanjuppun oki]
every hour	１時間に １回 [ichi jikan ni ittu kai]
several times a day	１日に数回 [ichi nichi ni sū kai]
… times a day	１日に…回 [ichi nichi ni … kai]
schedule	時刻表 [jikoku hyō]
Where can I see the schedule?	どこで時刻表を見られますか？ [doko de jikoku hyō wo mirare masu ka ?]
When is the next bus?	次のバスは何時ですか？ [tsugi no basu wa nan ji desu ka ?]
When is the first bus?	最初のバスは何時ですか？ [saisho no basu wa nan ji desu ka ?]
When is the last bus?	最後のバスは何時ですか？ [saigo no basu wa nan ji desu ka ?]

stop
バス停、停留所
[basutei, teiryūjo]

next stop
次のバス停、次の停留所
[tsugi no basutei, tsugi no teiryūjo]

last stop (terminus)
最終停留所
[saishū teiryūjo]

Stop here, please.
ここで止めてください。
[koko de tome te kudasai]

Excuse me, this is my stop.
すみません、ここで降ります。
[sumimasen, koko de ori masu]

Train

train	電車 [densha]
suburban train	郊外電車 [kōgai densha]
long-distance train	長距離列車 [chōkyori ressha]
train station	電車の駅 [densha no eki]
Excuse me, where is the exit to the platform?	すみません、ホームへはど う行けばいいですか？ [sumimasen, hōmu e wa dō ike ba ī desu ka?]
Does this train go to ...?	この電車は…まで行きますか？ [kono densha wa ... made iki masu ka ?]
next train	次の駅 [tsugi no eki]
When is the next train?	次の電車は何時ですか？ [tsugi no densha wa nan ji desu ka ?]
Where can I see the schedule?	どこで時刻表を見られますか？ [doko de jikoku hyō wo mirare masu ka ?]
From which platform?	どのホームからですか？ [dono hōmu kara desu ka ?]
When does the train arrive in ...?	電車はいつ到着しますか…？ [densha wa i tsu tōchaku shi masu ka ...?]
Please help me.	助けて下さい。 [tasuke te kudasai]
I'm looking for my seat.	私の座席を探しています。 [watashi no zaseki wo sagashi te i masu]
We're looking for our seats.	私たちの座席を探し ています。 [watashi tachi no zaseki wo sagashi te i masu]
My seat is taken.	私の席に他の人が 座っています。 [watashi no seki ni hoka no hito ga suwatte i masu]
Our seats are taken.	私たちの席に他の人が 座っています。 [watashi tachi no seki ni hoka no hito ga suwatte i masu.]

I'm sorry but this is my seat.

すみませんが、こちらは私
の席です。
[sumimasen ga, kochira wa watashi
no seki desu]

Is this seat taken?

この席はふさがっていますか？
[kono seki wa husagatte i masu ka ?]

May I sit here?

ここに座ってもいいですか？
[koko ni suwatte mo ī desu ka ?]

On the train. Dialogue (No ticket)

Ticket, please.	乗車券を見せて下さい。 [jōsha ken wo mise te kudasai]
I don't have a ticket.	乗車券を持っていません。 [jōsha ken wo motte i masen]
I lost my ticket.	乗車券を失くしました。 [jōsha ken wo nakushi mashi ta]
I forgot my ticket at home.	乗車券を家に忘れました。 [jōsha ken wo ie ni wasure mashi ta]
You can buy a ticket from me.	私からも乗車券を購入できます。 [watashi kara mo jōsha ken wo kōnyū deki masu]
You will also have to pay a fine.	それから罰金を払わなけれ ばいけません。 [sorekara bakkin wo harawa nakere ba ike masen]
Okay.	わかりました。 [wakari mashi ta]
Where are you going?	行き先はどこですか？ [yukisaki wa doko desu ka ?]
I'm going to ...	…に行きます。 [... ni iki masu]
How much? I don't understand.	いくらですか？ わかりません。 [ikura desu ka ? wakari masen]
Write it down, please.	書いてください。 [kai te kudasai]
Okay. Can I pay with a credit card?	わかりました。クレジットカード で支払いできますか？ [wakari mashi ta. kurejittokādo de shiharaideki masu ka?]
Yes, you can.	はい。 [hai]
Here's your receipt.	レシートです。 [reshīto desu]
Sorry about the fine.	罰金をいただいてすみません。 [bakkin wo itadaite sumimasen]
That's okay. It was my fault.	大丈夫です。私のせいですから。 [daijōbu desu. watashi no sei desu kara]
Enjoy your trip.	良い旅を。 [yoi tabi wo]

Taxi

taxi	タクシー [takushī]
taxi driver	タクシー運転手 [takushī unten shu]
to catch a taxi	タクシーをひろう [takushī wo hirō]
taxi stand	タクシー乗り場 [takushī noriba]
Where can I get a taxi?	どこでタクシーをひろえますか？ [doko de takushī wo hiroe masu ka ?]
to call a taxi	タクシーを呼ぶ [takushī wo yobu]
I need a taxi.	タクシーが必要です。 [takushī ga hitsuyō desu]
Right now.	今すぐ。 [ima sugu]
What is your address (location)?	住所はどこですか？ [jūsho wa doko desu ka ?]
My address is ...	私の住所は…です [watashi no jūsho wa ... desu]
Your destination?	どちらへ行かれますか？ [dochira e ikare masu ka ?]
Excuse me, ...	すみません、… [sumimasen, ...]
Are you available?	乗ってもいいですか？ [nottemo ī desu ka ?]
How much is it to get to ...?	…までいくらですか？ [... made ikura desu ka ?]
Do you know where it is?	どこにあるかご存知ですか？ [doko ni aru ka gozonji desu ka ?]
Airport, please.	空港へお願いします。 [kūkō e onegai shi masu]
Stop here, please.	ここで止めてください。 [koko de tome te kudasai]
It's not here.	ここではありません。 [koko de wa ari masen]
This is the wrong address.	その住所は間違っています。 [sono jūsho wa machigatte i masu]
Turn left.	左へ曲がって下さい [hidari e magatte kudasai]
Turn right.	右へ曲がって下さい [migi e magatte kudasai]

How much do I owe you?	いくらですか？ [ikura desu ka ?]
I'd like a receipt, please.	領収書を下さい。 [ryōshū sho wo kudasai]
Keep the change.	おつりはいりません。 [o tsuri hairi masen]

Would you please wait for me?	待っていて頂けますか？ [matte i te itadake masu ka?]
five minutes	5分 [go fun]
ten minutes	10分 [juppun]
fifteen minutes	15分 [jyū go fun]
twenty minutes	20分 [nijuppun]
half an hour	30分 [sanjuppun]

Hotel

Hello.	こんにちは。 [konnichiwa]
My name is ...	私の名前は…です [watashi no namae wa ... desu]
I have a reservation.	予約をしました。 [yoyaku wo shi mashi ta]
I need ...	私は…が必要です [watashi wa ... ga hitsuyō desu]
a single room	シングルルーム [shinguru rūmu]
a double room	ツインルーム [tsuin rūmu]
How much is that?	いくらですか? [ikura desu ka ?]
That's a bit expensive.	それは少し高いです。 [sore wa sukoshi takai desu]
Do you have any other options?	他にも選択肢はありますか? [hoka ni mo sentakushi wa ari masu ka ?]
I'll take it.	それにします。 [sore ni shi masu]
I'll pay in cash.	現金で払います。 [genkin de harai masu]
I've got a problem.	困ったことがあります。 [komatta koto ga arimasu]
My ... is broken.	私の…が壊れています。 [watashi no ... ga koware te i masu]
My ... is out of order.	私の…が故障しています。 [watashi no ... ga koshō shi te i masu]
TV	テレビ [terebi]
air conditioning	エアコン [eakon]
tap	蛇口 [jaguchi]
shower	シャワー [shawā]
sink	流し台 [nagashi dai]
safe	金庫 [kinko]

door lock	錠 [jō]
electrical outlet	電気のコンセント [dengen no konsento]
hairdryer	ドライヤー [doraiyā]

I don't have ...	…がありません [… ga ari masen]
water	水 [mizu]
light	明かり [akari]
electricity	電気 [denki]

Can you give me ...?	…を頂けませんか？ [… wo itadake masenka ?]
a towel	タオル [taoru]
a blanket	毛布 [mōfu]
slippers	スリッパ [surippa]
a robe	バスローブ [basurōbu]
shampoo	シャンプーを何本か [shanpū wo nannbon ka]
soap	石鹸をいくつか [sekken wo ikutsu ka]

I'd like to change rooms.	部屋を変えたいのですが。 [heya wo kae tai no desu ga]
I can't find my key.	鍵が見つかりません。 [kagi ga mitsukarimasenn]
Could you open my room, please?	部屋を開けて頂けますか？ [heya wo ake te itadake masu ka ?]
Who's there?	誰ですか？ [dare desu ka ?]
Come in!	どうぞお入り下さい [dōzo o hairikudasai]
Just a minute!	少々お待ち下さい！ [shōshō omachi kudasai !]
Not right now, please.	後にしてもらえますか。 [ato ni shi te morae masu ka]

Come to my room, please.	私の部屋に来て下さい。 [watashi no heya ni ki te kudasai]
I'd like to order food service.	食事サービスをお願いしたい のですが。 [shokuji sābisu wo onegai shi tai no desu ga]

My room number is …	私の部屋の番号は… [watashi no heya no bangō wa …]
I'm leaving …	チェックアウトします… [tyekkuauto shi masu …]
We're leaving …	私たちはチェックアウトします… [watashi tachi wa tyekkuauto shi masu …]
right now	今すぐ [ima sugu]
this afternoon	今日の午後 [kyō no gogo]
tonight	今晩 [konban]
tomorrow	明日 [ashita]
tomorrow morning	明日の朝 [ashita no asa]
tomorrow evening	明日の夕方 [ashita no yūgata]
the day after tomorrow	あさって [asatte]

I'd like to pay.	支払いをしたいのですが。 [shiharai wo shi tai no desu ga]
Everything was wonderful.	何もかもがよかったです。 [nanimokamo ga yokatta desu]
Where can I get a taxi?	どこでタクシーをひろえますか？ [doko de takushī wo hiroe masu ka ?]
Would you call a taxi for me, please?	タクシーを呼んでいただけますか？ [takushī wo yon de itadake masu ka ?]

Restaurant

Can I look at the menu, please?	メニューを頂けますか？ [menyū wo itadake masu ka ?]
Table for one.	一人用の席をお願いします。 [hitori yō no seki wo onegai shimasu]
There are two (three, four) of us.	2人（3人、4人）です。 [futari (san nin, yon nin) desu]

Smoking	喫煙 [kitsuen]
No smoking	禁煙 [kinen]
Excuse me! (addressing a waiter)	すみません！ [sumimasen !]
menu	メニュー [menyū]
wine list	ワインリスト [wain risuto]
The menu, please.	メニューを下さい。 [menyū wo kudasai]

Are you ready to order?	ご注文をお伺いしても よろしいですか？ [go chūmon wo o ukagai shi te mo yoroshī desu ka?]
What will you have?	ご注文は何にしますか？ [go chūmon wa nani ni shi masu ka ?]
I'll have …	…を下さい。 [… wo kudasai]

I'm a vegetarian.	私はベジタリアンです。 [watashi wa bejitarian desu]
meat	肉 [niku]
fish	魚 [sakana]
vegetables	野菜 [yasai]
Do you have vegetarian dishes?	ベジタリアン向けの料理はありますか？ [bejitarian muke no ryōri wa ari masu ka?]
I don't eat pork.	私は豚肉を食べません。 [watashi wa butaniku o tabe masen]

He /she/ doesn't eat meat.	彼 /彼女/ は肉を食べません。 [kare /kanojo/ wa niku o tabe masen]
I am allergic to ...	私は…にアレルギーがあります [watashi wa ... ni arerugī ga ari masu]
Would you please bring me ...	…を持ってきてもらえますか [... wo motte ki te morae masu ka]
salt | pepper | sugar	塩 | 胡椒 | 砂糖 [shio | koshō | satō]
coffee | tea | dessert	コーヒー | お茶 | デザート [kōhī | ocha | dezāto]
water | sparkling | plain	水 | スパークリングウォーター | 真水 [mizu | supāku ringu wōtā | mamizu]
a spoon | fork | knife	スプーン | フォーク | ナイフ [supūn | fōku | naifu]
a plate | napkin	プレート | ナプキン [purēto | napukin]

Enjoy your meal!	どうぞお召し上がりください [dōzo omeshiagari kudasai]
One more, please.	もう一つお願いします。 [mō hitotsu onegai shi masu]
It was very delicious.	とても美味しかったです。 [totemo oishikatta desu]

---

check | change | tip	勘定 | おつり | チップ [kanjō | o tsuri | chippu]
Check, please. (Could I have the check, please?)	お勘定をお願いします。 [o kanjō wo onegai shi masu]
Can I pay by credit card?	カードで支払いができますか？ [kādo de shiharai ga deki masu ka ?]
I'm sorry, there's a mistake here.	すみません、間違いがあります。 [sumimasen, machigai ga ari masu]

Shopping

Can I help you?	いらっしゃいませ。
	[irasshai mase]
Do you have ...?	…をお持ちですか？
	[... wo o mochi desu ka ?]
I'm looking for ...	…を探しています
	[... wo sagashi te i masu]
I need ...	…が必要です
	[... ga hitsuyō desu]

I'm just looking.	ただ見ているだけです。
	[tada mi te iru dake desu]
We're just looking.	私たちはただ見ているだけです。
	[watashi tachi wa tada mi te iru
	dake desu]

I'll come back later.	また後で来ます。
	[mata atode ki masu]
We'll come back later.	また後で来ます。
	[mata atode ki masu]
discounts	sale	値引き ｜ セール
	[nebiki	sēru]

Would you please show me ...	…を見せていただけますか
	[... wo mise te itadake masu ka]
Would you please give me ...	…をいただけますか
	[... wo itadake masu ka]
Can I try it on?	試着できますか？
	[shichaku deki masu ka ?]
Excuse me, where's the fitting room?	すみません、試着室は
	どこですか？
	[sumimasen, shichaku shitsu wa
	doko desu ka?]
Which color would you like?	どの色がお好みですか？
	[dono iro ga o konomi desu ka ?]
size	length	サイズ ｜ 長さ
	[saizu	naga sa]
How does it fit?	サイズは合いましたか？
	[saizu wa ai mashi ta ka ?]

How much is it?	これはいくらですか？
	[kore wa ikura desu ka ?]
That's too expensive.	高すぎます。
	[takasugi masu]

I'll take it.

これにします。
[kore ni shi masu]

Excuse me, where do I pay?

すみません、どこで支払いますか？
[sumimasen, doko de shiharai masu ka ?]

Will you pay in cash or credit card?

現金とクレジットカードのどちら
でお支払いされますか？
[genkin to kurejittokādo no dochira de o shiharai sare masu ka?]

In cash | with credit card

現金 ｜ クレジットカード
[genkin | kurejittokādo]

Do you want the receipt?

レシートはお入り用ですか？
[reshīto ha oiriyō desu ka ?]

Yes, please.

お願いします。
[onegai shi masu]

No, it's OK.

いえ、結構です。
[ie, kekkō desu]

Thank you. Have a nice day!

ありがとうございます。良い一日を！
[arigatō gozai masu. yoi ichi nichi wo !]

In town

Excuse me, please.	すみません、… [sumimasen, …]
I'm looking for …	…を探しています [watashi wa … wo sagashi te i masu]
the subway	地下鉄 [chikatetsu]
my hotel	ホテル [hoteru]
the movie theater	映画館 [eiga kan]
a taxi stand	タクシー乗り場 [takushī noriba]
an ATM	ＡＴＭ [ētīemu]
a foreign exchange office	両替所 [ryōgae sho]
an internet café	インターネットカフェ [intānetto kafe]
… street	…通り [… tōri]
this place	この場所 [kono basho]
Do you know where … is?	…がどこにあるかご存知ですか？ [… ga doko ni aru ka gozonji desu ka ?]
Which street is this?	この通りの名前は何ですか？ [kono michi no namae wa nani desu ka ?]
Show me where we are right now.	今どこにいるかを教えて下さい。 [ima doko ni iru ka wo oshie te kudasai]
Can I get there on foot?	そこまで歩いて行けますか？ [soko made arui te ike masu ka?]
Do you have a map of the city?	市内地図をお持ちですか？ [shinai chizu wo o mochi desu ka ?]
How much is a ticket to get in?	チケットはいくらですか？ [chiketto wa ikura desu ka ?]
Can I take pictures here?	ここで写真を撮ってもいいですか？ [koko de shashin wo totte mo ī desu ka ?]
Are you open?	開いていますか？ [hirai te i masu ka ?]

When do you open?

何時に開きますか？
[nan ji ni hiraki masu ka ?]

When do you close?

何時に閉まりますか？
[nan ji ni shimari masu ka ?]

Money

money	お金 [okane]
cash	現金 [genkin]
paper money	紙幣 [shihei]
loose change	おつり [o tsuri]
check | change | tip	勘定 ｜ おつり ｜ チップ [kanjō | o tsuri | chippu]
credit card	クレジットカード [kurejittokādo]
wallet	財布 [saifu]
to buy	買う [kau]
to pay	支払う [shiharau]
fine	罰金 [bakkin]
free	無料 [muryō]
Where can I buy ...?	…はどこで買えますか？ [... wa doko de kae masu ka ?]
Is the bank open now?	銀行は今開いていますか？ [ginkō wa ima hirai te i masu ka ?]
When does it open?	いつ開きますか？ [itsu hiraki masu ka ?]
When does it close?	いつ閉まりますか？ [itsu shimari masu ka ?]
How much?	いくらですか？ [ikura desu ka ?]
How much is this?	これはいくらですか？ [kore wa ikura desu ka ?]
That's too expensive.	高すぎます。 [takasugi masu]
Excuse me, where do I pay?	すみません、レジはどこですか？ [sumimasen, reji wa doko desu ka ?]
Check, please.	勘定をお願いします。 [kanjō wo onegai shi masu]

Can I pay by credit card?　　　　　カードで支払いができますか？
[kādo de shiharai ga deki masu ka ?]

Is there an ATM here?　　　　　　ここにＡＴＭはありますか？
[kokoni ētīemu wa ari masu ka ?]

I'm looking for an ATM.　　　　　ＡＴＭを探しています。
[ētīemu wo sagashi te i masu]

I'm looking for a foreign exchange office.　両替所を探しています。
[ryōgae sho wo sagashi te i masu]

I'd like to change …　　　　　　両替をしたいのですが…
[ryōgae wo shi tai no desu ga…]

What is the exchange rate?　　　　為替レートはいくらですか？
[kawase rēto wa ikura desu ka ?]

Do you need my passport?　　　　パスポートは必要ですか？
[pasupōto ha hituyō desu ka ?]

Time

What time is it?	何時ですか？ [nan ji desu ka ?]
When?	いつですか？ [i tsu desu ka ?]
At what time?	何時にですか？ [nan ji ni desu ka ?]
now | later | after ...	今 ｜ 1後で ｜ …の後 [ima ｜ato de ｜ … no ato]
one o'clock	1時 [ichi ji]
one fifteen	1時 15分 [ichi ji jyū go fun]
one thirty	1時半 [ichi ji han]
one forty-five	1時45分 [ichi ji yon jyū go fun]
one | two | three	1 ｜ 2 ｜ 3 [ichi ｜ ni ｜ san]
four | five | six	4 ｜ 5 ｜ 6 [yonn ｜ go ｜roku]
seven | eight | nine	7 ｜ 8 ｜ 9 [shichi ｜ hachi ｜ kyū]
ten | eleven | twelve	10 ｜ 11 ｜ 12 [jyū ｜ jyūichi ｜ jyūni]
in ...	…後 [… go]
five minutes	5分 [go fun]
ten minutes	10分 [juppun]
fifteen minutes	15分 [jyū go fun]
twenty minutes	20分 [nijuppun]
half an hour	30分 [sanjuppun]
an hour	一時間 [ichi jikan]

in the morning	朝に [asa ni]
early in the morning	早朝 [sōchō]
this morning	今朝 [kesa]
tomorrow morning	明日の朝 [ashita no asa]
at noon	ランチのときに [ranchi no toki ni]
in the afternoon	午後に [gogo ni]
in the evening	夕方 [yūgata]
tonight	今夜 [konya]
at night	夜 [yoru]
yesterday	昨日 [kinō]
today	今日 [kyō]
tomorrow	明日 [ashita]
the day after tomorrow	あさって [asatte]
What day is it today?	今日は何曜日ですか？ [kyō wa nan yōbi desu ka ?]
It's ...	…です [… desu]
Monday	月曜日 [getsuyōbi]
Tuesday	火曜日 [kayōbi]
Wednesday	水曜日 [suiyōbi]
Thursday	木曜日 [mokuyōbi]
Friday	金曜日 [kinyōbi]
Saturday	土曜日 [doyōbi]
Sunday	日曜日 [nichiyōbi]

Greetings. Introductions

Hello.	こんにちは。 [konnichiwa]
Pleased to meet you.	お会いできて嬉しいです。 [o aideki te ureshī desu]
Me too.	こちらこそ。 [kochira koso]
I'd like you to meet ...	…さんに会わせていただきたいのですが [... san ni awasete itadaki tai no desu ga]
Nice to meet you.	初めまして。 [hajime mashite]

How are you?	お元気ですか？ [o genki desu ka ?]
My name is ...	私の名前は…です [watashi no namae wa ... desu]
His name is ...	彼の名前は…です [kare no namae wa ... desu]
Her name is ...	彼女の名前は…です [kanojo no namae wa ... desu]
What's your name?	お名前は何ですか？ [o namae wa nan desu ka ?]
What's his name?	彼の名前は何ですか？ [kare no namae wa nan desu ka ?]
What's her name?	彼女の名前は何ですか？ [kanojo no namae wa nan desu ka ?]

What's your last name?	苗字は何ですか？ [myōji wa nan desu ka ?]
You can call me ...	…と呼んで下さい [... to yon de kudasai]
Where are you from?	ご出身はどちらですか？ [go shusshin wa dochira desu ka ?]
I'm from ...	…の出身です [... no shusshin desu]
What do you do for a living?	お仕事は何をされていますか？ [o shigoto wa nani wo sare te i masu ka ?]
Who is this?	誰ですか？ [dare desu ka ?]
Who is he?	彼は誰ですか？ [kare wa dare desu ka ?]
Who is she?	彼女は誰ですか？ [kanojo wa dare desu ka ?]
Who are they?	彼らは誰ですか？ [karera wa dare desu ka ?]

This is ...	こちらは… [kochira wa …]
my friend (masc.)	私の友達です [watashi no tomodachi desu]
my friend (fem.)	私の友達です [watashi no tomodachi desu]
my husband	私の主人です [watashi no shujin desu]
my wife	私の妻です [watashi no tsuma desu]
my father	私の父です [watashi no chichi desu]
my mother	私の母です [watashi no haha desu]
my brother	私の兄です [watashi no ani desu]
my sister	私の妹です [watashi no imōto desu]
my son	私の息子です [watashi no musuko desu]
my daughter	私の娘です [watashi no musume desu]
This is our son.	私たちの息子です。 [watashi tachi no musuko desu]
This is our daughter.	私たちの娘です。 [watashi tachi no musume desu]
These are my children.	私の子供です。 [watashi no kodomo desu]
These are our children.	私たちの子供です。 [watashi tachi no kodomo desu]

Farewells

Good bye!	さようなら！ [sayōnara !]
Bye! (inform.)	じゃあね！ [jā ne !]
See you tomorrow.	また明日。 [mata ashita]
See you soon.	またね。 [mata ne]
See you at seven.	7時に会おう。 [shichi ji ni ao u]
Have fun!	楽しんでね！ [tanoshin de ne !]
Talk to you later.	じゃあ後で。 [jā atode]
Have a nice weekend.	良い週末を。 [yoi shūmatsu wo]
Good night.	お休みなさい。 [o yasuminasai]
It's time for me to go.	もう時間です。 [mō jikan desu]
I have to go.	もう行かなければなりません。 [mō ika nakere ba nari masen]
I will be right back.	すぐ戻ります。 [sugu modori masu]
It's late.	もう遅いです。 [mō osoi desu]
I have to get up early.	早く起きなければいけません。 [hayaku oki nakere ba ike masen]
I'm leaving tomorrow.	明日出発します。 [ashita shuppatsu shi masu]
We're leaving tomorrow.	私たちは明日出発します。 [watashi tachi wa ashita shuppatsu shi masu]
Have a nice trip!	旅行を楽しんで下さい！ [ryokō wo tanoshin de kudasai !]
It was nice meeting you.	お会いできて嬉しかったです。 [o shiriai ni nare te uresikatta desu]
It was nice talking to you.	お話できて良かったです。 [ohanashi deki te yokatta desu]

Thanks for everything.
色々とありがとうございました。
[iroiro to arigatō gozai mashi ta]

I had a very good time.
とても楽しかったです。
[totemo tanoshikatta desu]

We had a very good time.
とても楽しかったです。
[totemo tanoshikatta desu]

It was really great.
とても楽しかった。
[totemo tanoshikatta]

I'm going to miss you.
寂しくなります。
[sabishiku nari masu]

We're going to miss you.
寂しくなります。
[sabishiku nari masu]

Good luck!
幸運を祈るよ！
[kōun wo inoru yo !]

Say hi to …
…に宜しくお伝え下さい。
[… ni yoroshiku otsutae kudasai]

Foreign language

I don't understand.	分かりません。 [wakari masen]
Write it down, please.	それを書いて頂けますか？ [sore wo kai te itadake masu ka ?]
Do you speak ...?	…語で話せますか？ [… go de hanase masu ka ?]

I speak a little bit of ...	…を少し話せます […wo sukoshi hanase masu]
English	英語 [eigo]
Turkish	トルコ語 [toruko go]
Arabic	アラビア語 [arabia go]
French	フランス語 [furansu go]

German	ドイツ語 [doitsu go]
Italian	イタリア語 [itaria go]
Spanish	スペイン語 [supein go]
Portuguese	ポルトガル語 [porutogaru go]
Chinese	中国語 [chūgoku go]
Japanese	日本語 [nihon go]

Can you repeat that, please.	もう一度言っていただけますか。 [mōichido itte itadake masuka]
I understand.	分かりました。 [wakari mashi ta]
I don't understand.	分かりません。 [wakari masen]
Please speak more slowly.	もう少しゆっくり話して下さい。 [mōsukoshi yukkuri hanashi te kudasai]

Is that correct? (Am I saying it right?)	これで合っていますか？ [kore de atte i masu ka ?]
What is this? (What does this mean?)	これは何ですか？ [kore wa nan desu ka ?]

Apologies

Excuse me, please.	すみませんがお願いします。 [sumimasen ga onegai shi masu]
I'm sorry.	ごめんなさい。 [gomennasai]
I'm really sorry.	本当にごめんなさい。 [hontōni gomennasai]
Sorry, it's my fault.	ごめんなさい、私のせいです。 [gomennasai, watashi no sei desu]
My mistake.	私の間違いでした。 [watashi no machigai deshi ta]
May I ...?	…してもいいですか？ [… shi te mo ī desu ka ?]
Do you mind if I ...?	…してもよろしいですか？ [… shi te mo yoroshī desu ka ?]
It's OK.	構いません。 [kamai masen]
It's all right.	大丈夫です。 [daijōbu desu]
Don't worry about it.	それについては心配しないで下さい。 [sore ni tuitewa shinpai shi nai de kudasai]

Agreement

Yes.	はい。 [hai]
Yes, sure.	はい、もちろん。 [hai, mochiron]
OK (Good!)	わかりました。 [wakari mashi ta]
Very well.	いいですよ。 [ī desuyo]
Certainly!	もちろん！ [mochiron !]
I agree.	賛成です。 [sansei desu]
That's correct.	それは正しい。 [sore wa tadashī]
That's right.	それは正しい。 [sore wa tadashī]
You're right.	あなたは合っています。 [anata wa atte imasu]
I don't mind.	気にしていません。 [kinisite imasen]
Absolutely right.	完全に正しいです。 [kanzen ni tadashī desu]
It's possible.	それは可能です。 [sore wa kanō desu]
That's a good idea.	それはいい考えです。 [sore wa ī kangae desu]
I can't say no.	断ることができません。 [kotowaru koto ga deki masen]
I'd be happy to.	喜んで。 [yorokon de]
With pleasure.	喜んで。 [yorokon de]

Refusal. Expressing doubt

No.
いいえ。
[īe]

Certainly not.
もちろん、違います。
[mochiron, chigai masu]

I don't agree.
賛成できません。
[sansei deki masen]

I don't think so.
そうは思いません。
[sō wa omoi masen]

It's not true.
それは事実ではありません。
[sore wa jijitsu de wa ari masen]

You are wrong.
あなたは間違っています。
[anata wa machigatte i masu]

I think you are wrong.
あなたは間違っていると思います。
[anata wa machigatte iru to omoi masu]

I'm not sure.
わかりません。
[wakari masen]

It's impossible.
それは不可能です。
[sore wa fukanō desu]

Nothing of the kind (sort)!
まさか！
[masaka !]

The exact opposite.
全く反対です。
[mattaku hantai desu]

I'm against it.
反対です。
[hantai desu]

I don't care.
構いません。
[kamai masen]

I have no idea.
全く分かりません。
[mattaku wakari masen]

I doubt that.
それはどうでしょう。
[sore wa dō desyō]

Sorry, I can't.
申し訳ありませんが、できません。
[mōshiwake arimasenga, deki masen]

Sorry, I don't want to.
申し訳ありませんが、遠慮させて
いただきたいのです。
[mōshiwake arimasenga, ennryosasete
itadakitai no desu]

Thank you, but I don't need this.
ありがとうございます。でもそれは
必要ではありません。
[arigatō gozai masu. demo sore wa
hitsuyō de wa ari masen]

It's late.

もう遅いです。
[mō osoi desu]

I have to get up early.

早く起きなければいけません。
[hayaku oki nakere ba ike masen]

I don't feel well.

気分が悪いのです。
[kibun ga warui nodesu]

Expressing gratitude

Thank you.　ありがとうございます。
[arigatō gozai masu]

Thank you very much.　どうもありがとうございます。
[dōmo arigatō gozai masu]

I really appreciate it.　本当に感謝しています。
[hontōni kansha shi te i masu]

I'm really grateful to you.　あなたに本当に感謝しています。
[anata ni hontōni kansha shi te i masu]

We are really grateful to you.　私たちはあなたに本当に
感謝しています。
[watashi tachi wa anata ni hontōni
kansha shi te i masu]

Thank you for your time.　お時間を頂きましてありがとう
ございました。
[o jikan wo itadaki mashi te arigatō
gozai mashi ta]

Thanks for everything.　何もかもありがとうございました。
[nanimokamo arigatō gozai mashi ta]

Thank you for ...　…をありがとうございます
[… wo arigatō gozai masu]

your help　助けて頂いて
[tasuke te itadai te]

a nice time　すばらしい時間
[subarashī jikan]

a wonderful meal　素敵なお料理
[suteki na o ryōri]

a pleasant evening　楽しい夜
[tanoshī yoru]

a wonderful day　素晴らしい 1 日
[subarashī ichinichi]

an amazing journey　楽しい旅
[tanoshī tabi]

Don't mention it.　どういたしまして。
[dōitashimashite]

You are welcome.　どういたしまして。
[dōitashimashite]

Any time.　いつでもどうぞ。
[itsu demo dōzo]

My pleasure.　どういたしまして。
[dōitashimashite]

Forget it. It's alright.　　　　　　忘れて下さい。
　　　　　　　　　　　　　　　　[wasure te kudasai]

Don't worry about it.　　　　　　心配しないで下さい。
　　　　　　　　　　　　　　　　[shinpai shi nai de kudasai]

Congratulations. Best wishes

Congratulations!
おめでとうございます！
[omedetō gozai masu !]

Happy birthday!
お誕生日おめでとうございます！
[o tanjō bi omedetō gozai masu !]

Merry Christmas!
メリークリスマス！
[merīkurisumasu !]

Happy New Year!
新年明けましておめでとう
ございます！
[shinnen ake mashi te omedetō
gozai masu !]

Happy Easter!
イースターおめでとうございます！
[īsutā omedetō gozai masu !]

Happy Hanukkah!
ハヌカおめでとうございます！
[hanuka omedetō gozai masu !]

I'd like to propose a toast.
乾杯をあげたいです。
[kanpai wo age tai desu]

Cheers!
乾杯！
[kanpai !]

Let's drink to ...!
…のために乾杯しましょう！
[... no tame ni kanpai shi masho u !]

To our success!
我々の成功のために！
[wareware no seikō no tame ni !]

To your success!
あなたの成功のために！
[anata no seikō no tame ni !]

Good luck!
幸運を祈るよ！
[kōun wo inoru yo !]

Have a nice day!
良い一日をお過ごし下さい！
[yoi ichi nichi wo osugoshi kudasai !]

Have a good holiday!
良い休日をお過ごし下さい！
[yoi kyūjitsu wo osugoshi kudasai !]

Have a safe journey!
道中ご無事で！
[dōtyū gobujide!]

I hope you get better soon!
早く良くなるといいですね！
[hayaku yoku naru to ī desu ne !]

Socializing

Why are you sad?　なぜ悲しいのですか？
[naze kanashī no desu ka ?]

Smile! Cheer up!　笑って！　元気を出してください！
[waratte ! genki wo dashite kudasai !]

Are you free tonight?　今夜あいていますか？
[konya ai te i masu ka ?]

May I offer you a drink?　何か飲みますか？
[nani ka nomi masu ka ?]

Would you like to dance?　踊りませんか？
[odori masen ka ?]

Let's go to the movies.　映画に行きましょう。
[eiga ni iki masho u]

May I invite you to ...?　…へ誘ってもいいですか？
[... e sasotte mo ī desu ka ?]

a restaurant　レストラン
[resutoran]

the movies　映画
[eiga]

the theater　劇場
[gekijō]

go for a walk　散歩
[sanpo]

At what time?　何時に？
[nan ji ni ?]

tonight　今晩
[konban]

at six　6時
[roku ji]

at seven　7時
[shichi ji]

at eight　8時
[hachi ji]

at nine　9時
[kyū ji]

Do you like it here?　ここが好きですか？
[koko ga suki desu ka ?]

Are you here with someone?　ここで誰かと一緒ですか？
[koko de dare ka to issyodesu ka ?]

I'm with my friend.　友達と一緒です。
[tomodachi to issho desu]

I'm with my friends.	友人たちと一緒です。 [yūjin tachi to issho desu]
No, I'm alone.	いいえ、一人です。 [īe, hitori desu]

Do you have a boyfriend?	彼氏いるの？ [kareshi iru no ?]
I have a boyfriend.	私は彼氏がいます。 [watashi wa kareshi ga i masu]
Do you have a girlfriend?	彼女いるの？ [kanojo iru no ?]
I have a girlfriend.	私は彼女がいます。 [watashi wa kanojo ga i masu]

Can I see you again?	また会えるかな？ [mata aeru ka na ?]
Can I call you?	電話してもいい？ [denwa shi te mo ī ?]
Call me. (Give me a call.)	電話してね。 [denwa shi te ne]
What's your number?	電話番号は？ [denwa bangō wa ?]
I miss you.	寂しくなるよ。 [sabishiku naru yo]

You have a beautiful name.	綺麗なお名前ですね。 [kirei na o namae desu ne]
I love you.	愛しているよ。 [aishi te iru yo]
Will you marry me?	結婚しようか [kekkon shiyo u ka]
You're kidding!	冗談でしょう！ [jōdan dessyō!]
I'm just kidding.	冗談だよ。 [jōdan da yo]

Are you serious?	本気ですか？ [honki desuka ?]
I'm serious.	本気です。 [honki desu]
Really?!	本当ですか？！ [hontō desu ka ?!]
It's unbelievable!	信じられません！ [shinjirare masen !]
I don't believe you.	あなたは信じられません。 [anata wa shinzirare masen]
I can't.	私にはできません。 [watashi ni wa deki masen]
I don't know.	わかりません。 [wakari masen]
I don't understand you.	おっしゃることが分かりません。 [ossharu koto ga wakari masen]

Please go away.

出ていって下さい。
[de te itte kudasai]

Leave me alone!

ほっといて下さい！
[hottoi te kudasai !]

I can't stand him.

彼には耐えられない。
[kare ni wa taerare nai]

You are disgusting!

いやな人ですね！
[iyana hito desu ne !]

I'll call the police!

警察を呼びますよ！
[keisatsu wo yobi masuyo !]

Sharing impressions. Emotions

I like it.	これが好きです。 [kore ga suki desu]
Very nice.	とても素晴らしい。 [totemo subarashī]
That's great!	それはすばらしいです！ [sore wa subarashī desu !]
It's not bad.	それは悪くはないです。 [sore wa waruku wa nai desu]
I don't like it.	それが好きではありません。 [sore ga suki de wa ari masen]
It's not good.	それはよくないです。 [sore wa yoku nai desu]
It's bad.	それはひどいです。 [sore wa hidoi desu]
It's very bad.	それはとてもひどいです。 [sore wa totemo hidoi desu]
It's disgusting.	それは最悪です。 [sore wa saiaku desu]
I'm happy.	幸せです。 [shiawase desu]
I'm content.	満足しています。 [manzoku shi te i masu]
I'm in love.	好きな人がいます。 [suki na hito ga i masu]
I'm calm.	冷静です。 [reisei desu]
I'm bored.	退屈です。 [taikutsu desu]
I'm tired.	疲れています。 [tsukare te i masu]
I'm sad.	悲しいです。 [kanashī desu]
I'm frightened.	怖いです。 [kowai desu]
I'm angry.	腹が立ちます。 [haraga tachi masu]
I'm worried.	心配しています。 [shinpai shi te i masu]
I'm nervous.	緊張しています。 [kinchō shi te i masu]

I'm jealous. (envious)   嫉妬しています。
[shitto shi te i masu]

I'm surprised.   驚いています。
[odoroi te i masu]

I'm perplexed.   恥ずかしいです。
[hazukashī desu]

Problems. Accidents

I've got a problem.
困っています。
[komatte imasu]

We've got a problem.
困っています。
[komatte imasu]

I'm lost.
道に迷いました。
[michi ni mayoi mashi ta]

I missed the last bus (train).
最終バス（電車）を逃しました。
[saishūbasu (densha) wo nogashi mashi ta]

I don't have any money left.
もうお金がありません。
[mō okane ga ari masen]

I've lost my ...
…を失くしました
[… wo nakushi mashi ta]

Someone stole my ...
…を盗まれました
[… wo nusumare mashi ta]

passport
パスポート
[pasupōto]

wallet
財布
[saifu]

papers
書類
[shorui]

ticket
切符
[kippu]

money
お金
[okane]

handbag
ハンドバック
[handobakku]

camera
カメラ
[kamera]

laptop
ノートパソコン
[nōto pasokon]

tablet computer
タブレット型コンピューター
[taburetto gata konpyūtā]

mobile phone
携帯電話
[keitai denwa]

Help me!
助けて下さい！
[tasuke te kudasai !]

What's happened?
どうしましたか？
[dō shi mashi ta ka ?]

fire	火災 [kasai]
shooting	発砲 [happō]
murder	殺人 [satsujin]
explosion	爆発 [bakuhatsu]
fight	けんか [kenka]

Call the police!	警察を呼んで下さい！ [keisatsu wo yon de kudasai !]
Please hurry up!	急いで下さい！ [isoi de kudasai !]
I'm looking for the police station.	警察署を探しています。 [keisatsu sho wo sagashi te imasu]
I need to make a call.	電話をしなければなりません。 [denwa wo shi nakere ba nari masen]
May I use your phone?	お電話をお借りしても良いですか？ [o denwa wo o karishi te mo ī desu ka ?]

I've been ...	…されました [... sare mashi ta]
mugged	強盗 [gōtō]
robbed	盗まれる [nusumareru]
raped	レイプ [reipu]
attacked (beaten up)	暴行される [bōkō sareru]

Are you all right?	大丈夫ですか？ [daijōbu desu ka ?]
Did you see who it was?	誰が犯人か見ましたか？ [dare ga hanninn ka mi mashi ta ka ?]
Would you be able to recognize the person?	その人がどんな人か 分かりますか？ [sono hito ga donna hito ka wakari masu ka?]
Are you sure?	本当に大丈夫ですか？ [hontōni daijōbu desu ka ?]

Please calm down.	落ち着いて下さい。 [ochitsui te kudasai]
Take it easy!	気楽に！ [kiraku ni !]
Don't worry!	心配しないで！ [shinpai shi nai de !]
Everything will be fine.	大丈夫ですから。 [daijōbu desu kara]

Everything's all right.
大丈夫ですから。
[daijōbu desu kara]

Come here, please.
こちらに来て下さい。
[kochira ni ki te kudasai]

I have some questions for you.
いくつかお伺いしたいことがあります。
[ikutuka o ukagai shi tai koto ga ari masu]

Wait a moment, please.
少しお待ち下さい。
[sukoshi omachi kudasai]

Do you have any I.D.?
身分証明書はお持ちですか？
[mibun shōmei sho wa o mochi desu ka ?]

Thanks. You can leave now.
ありがとうございます。もう
行っていいですよ。
[arigatō gozai masu. mō
itte ī desuyo]

Hands behind your head!
両手を頭の後ろで組みなさい！
[ryōute wo atama
no ushiro de kuminasai !]

You're under arrest!
逮捕します
[taiho shi masu]

Health problems

Please help me.	助けて下さい。 [tasuke te kudasai]
I don't feel well.	気分が悪いのです。 [kibun ga warui nodesu]
My husband doesn't feel well.	主人の具合が悪いのです。 [shujin no guai ga warui no desu]
My son ...	息子の… [musuko no …]
My father ...	父の… [chichi no …]
My wife doesn't feel well.	妻の具合が悪いのです。 [tsuma no guai ga warui no desu]
My daughter ...	娘の… [musume no …]
My mother ...	母の… [haha no …]
I've got a ...	…がします [… ga shi masu]
headache	頭痛 [zutsū]
sore throat	喉が痛い [nodo ga itai]
stomach ache	腹痛 [fukutsū]
toothache	歯痛 [shitsū]
I feel dizzy.	めまいがします。 [memai ga shi masu]
He has a fever.	彼は熱があります。 [kare wa netsu ga ari masu]
She has a fever.	彼女は熱があります。 [kanojo wa netsu ga ari masu]
I can't breathe.	息ができません。 [iki ga deki masen]
I'm short of breath.	息切れがします。 [ikigire ga shi masu]
I am asthmatic.	喘息です。 [zensoku desu]
I am diabetic.	糖尿病です。 [tōnyō byō desu]

I can't sleep.　不眠症です。
[huminsyō desu]

food poisoning　食中毒
[shokuchūdoku]

It hurts here.　ここが痛いです。
[koko ga itai desu]

Help me!　助けて下さい！
[tasuke te kudasai !]

I am here!　ここにいます！
[koko ni i masu !]

We are here!　私たちはここにいます！
[watashi tachi wa koko ni i masu !]

Get me out of here!　ここから出して下さい！
[koko kara dashi te kudasai !]

I need a doctor.　医者に診せる必要があります。
[isha ni miseru hituyō ga arimasu]

I can't move.　動けません！
[ugoke masen !]

I can't move my legs.　足が動きません。
[ashi ga ugoki masen]

I have a wound.　傷があります。
[kizu ga ari masu]

Is it serious?　それは重傷ですか？
[sore wa jūsyō desu ka ?]

My documents are in my pocket.　私に関する書類はポケッ
トに入っています。
[watashi nikansuru shorui wa poketto
ni haitte i masu]

Calm down!　落ち着いて下さい！
[ochitsui te kudasai !]

May I use your phone?　お電話をお借りしても良いですか？
[o denwa wo o karishi te mo ī desu ka ?]

Call an ambulance!　救急車を呼んで下さい！
[kyūkyū sha wo yon de kudasai !]

It's urgent!　緊急です！
[kinkyū desu !]

It's an emergency!　緊急です！
[kinkyū desu !]

Please hurry up!　急いで下さい！
[isoi de kudasai !]

Would you please call a doctor?　医者を呼んでいただけますか？
[isha wo yon de itadake masu ka ?]

Where is the hospital?　病院はどこですか？
[byōin wa doko desu ka ?]

How are you feeling?　ご気分はいかがですか？
[gokibun wa ikaga desu ka ?]

Are you all right?　大丈夫ですか？
[daijōbu desu ka ?]

What's happened?	どうしましたか？ [dō shi mashi ta ka ?]
I feel better now.	もう気分が良くなりました。 [mō kibun ga yoku narimashita]
It's OK.	大丈夫です。 [daijōbu desu]
It's all right.	大丈夫です。 [daijōbu desu]

At the pharmacy

pharmacy (drugstore)	薬局 [yakkyoku]
24-hour pharmacy	２４時間営業の薬局 [nijyū yo jikan eigyō no yakkyoku]
Where is the closest pharmacy?	一番近くの薬局はどこですか？ [ichiban chikaku no yakkyoku wa doko desu ka?]
Is it open now?	今開いていますか？ [ima ai te i masu ka ?]
At what time does it open?	何時に開きますか？ [nan ji ni aki masu ka ?]
At what time does it close?	何時に閉まりますか？ [nan ji ni shimari masu ka ?]
Is it far?	遠いですか？ [tōi desu ka ?]
Can I get there on foot?	そこまで歩いて行けますか？ [soko made arui te ike masu ka ?]
Can you show me on the map?	地図で教えて頂けますか？ [chizu de oshie te itadake masu ka ?]
Please give me something for ...	何か…に効くものを下さい [nani ka ... ni kiku mono wo kudasai]
a headache	頭痛 [zutsū]
a cough	咳 [seki]
a cold	風邪 [kaze]
the flu	インフルエンザ [infuruenza]
a fever	発熱 [hatsunetsu]
a stomach ache	胃痛 [itsū]
nausea	吐き気 [hakike]
diarrhea	下痢 [geri]
constipation	便秘 [benpi]

pain in the back	腰痛 [yōtsū]
chest pain	胸痛 [kyōtsū]
side stitch	脇腹の痛み [wakibara no itami]
abdominal pain	腹痛 [fukutsū]

pill	薬 [kusuri]
ointment, cream	軟膏、クリーム [nankō, kurīmu]
syrup	シロップ [shiroppu]
spray	スプレー [supurē]
drops	目薬 [megusuri]

You need to go to the hospital.	病院に行かなくてはなりません。 [byōin ni ika naku te wa nari masen]
health insurance	健康保険 [kenkō hoken]
prescription	処方箋 [shohōsen]
insect repellant	虫除け [mushiyoke]
Band Aid	絆創膏 [bansōkō]

The bare minimum

Excuse me, ...	すみません、… [sumimasen, ...]
Hello.	こんにちは。 [konnichiwa]
Thank you.	ありがとうございます。 [arigatō gozai masu]
Good bye.	さようなら。 [sayōnara]
Yes.	はい。 [hai]
No.	いいえ。 [īe]
I don't know.	わかりません。 [wakari masen]
Where? | Where to? | When?	どこ？ | どこへ？ | いつ？ [doko ? | doko e ? | i tsu ?]

I need ...	…が必要です [... ga hitsuyō desu]
I want ...	したいです [shi tai desu]
Do you have ...?	…をお持ちですか？ [... wo o mochi desu ka ?]
Is there a ... here?	ここには…がありますか？ [koko ni wa ... ga ari masu ka ?]
May I ...?	…してもいいですか？ [... shi te mo ī desu ka ?]
..., please (polite request)	お願いします。 [onegai shi masu]

I'm looking for ...	…を探しています [... wo sagashi te i masu]
restroom	トイレ [toire]
ATM	ＡＴＭ [ētīemu]
pharmacy (drugstore)	薬局 [yakkyoku]
hospital	病院 [byōin]
police station	警察 [keisatsu]
subway	地下鉄 [chikatetsu]

taxi	タクシー [takushī]
train station	駅 [eki]

My name is ...	私は…と申します [watashi wa … to mōshi masu]
What's your name?	お名前は何ですか？ [o namae wa nan desu ka ?]
Could you please help me?	助けていただけますか？ [tasuke te itadake masu ka ?]
I've got a problem.	困ったことがあります。 [komatta koto ga arimasu]
I don't feel well.	気分が悪いのです。 [kibun ga warui nodesu]
Call an ambulance!	救急車を呼んで下さい！ [kyūkyū sha wo yon de kudasai !]
May I make a call?	電話をしてもいいですか？ [denwa wo shi te mo ī desu ka ?]

I'm sorry.	ごめんなさい。 [gomennasai]
You're welcome.	どういたしまして。 [dōitashimashite]

I, me	私 [watashi]
you (inform.)	君 [kimi]
he	彼 [kare]
she	彼女 [kanojo]
they (masc.)	彼ら [karera]
they (fem.)	彼女たち [kanojotachi]
we	私たち [watashi tachi]
you (pl)	君たち [kimi tachi]
you (sg, form.)	あなた [anata]

ENTRANCE	入り口 [iriguchi]
EXIT	出口 [deguchi]
OUT OF ORDER	故障中 [koshō chū]
CLOSED	休業中 [kyūgyō chū]

OPEN

営業中
[eigyō chū]

FOR WOMEN

女性用
[josei yō]

FOR MEN

男性用
[dansei yō]

CONCISE DICTIONARY

This section contains more than 1,500 useful words arranged alphabetically. The dictionary includes a lot of gastronomic terms and will be helpful when ordering food at a restaurant or buying groceries

T&P Books Publishing

DICTIONARY CONTENTS

T&P Books Publishing

T&P Books Publishing

1. Time. Calendar

time	時間	jikan
hour	時間	jikan
half an hour	３０分	san jū fun
minute	分	fun, pun
second	秒	byō
today (adv)	今日	kyō
tomorrow (adv)	明日	ashita
yesterday (adv)	昨日	kinō
Monday	月曜日	getsuyōbi
Tuesday	火曜日	kayōbi
Wednesday	水曜日	suiyōbi
Thursday	木曜日	mokuyōbi
Friday	金曜日	kinyōbi
Saturday	土曜日	doyōbi
Sunday	日曜日	nichiyōbi
day	日	nichi
working day	営業日	eigyōbi
public holiday	公休	kōkyū
weekend	週末	shūmatsu
week	週	shū
last week (adv)	先週	senshū
next week (adv)	来週	raishū
sunrise	日の出	hinode
sunset	夕日	yūhi
in the morning	朝に	asa ni
in the afternoon	午後に	gogo ni
in the evening	夕方に	yūgata ni
tonight (this evening)	今夜	konya
at night	夜に	yoru ni
midnight	真夜中	mayonaka
January	一月	ichigatsu
February	二月	nigatsu
March	三月	sangatsu
April	四月	shigatsu
May	五月	gogatsu
June	六月	rokugatsu

July	七月	shichigatsu
August	八月	hachigatsu
September	九月	kugatsu
October	十月	jūgatsu
November	十一月	jūichigatsu
December	十二月	jūnigatsu

in spring	春に	haru ni
in summer	夏に	natsu ni
in fall	秋に	aki ni
in winter	冬に	fuyu ni

month	月	tsuki
season (summer, etc.)	季節	kisetsu
year	年	nen
century	世紀	seiki

2. Numbers. Numerals

digit, figure	桁数	keta sū
number	数字	sūji
minus sign	負号	fugō
plus sign	正符号	sei fugō
sum, total	合計	gōkei

first (adj)	第一の	dai ichi no
second (adj)	第二の	dai ni no
third (adj)	第三の	dai san no

0 zero	ゼロ	zero
1 one	一	ichi
2 two	二	ni
3 three	三	san
4 four	四	yon

5 five	五	go
6 six	六	roku
7 seven	七	nana
8 eight	八	hachi
9 nine	九	kyū
10 ten	十	jū

11 eleven	十一	jū ichi
12 twelve	十二	jū ni
13 thirteen	十三	jū san
14 fourteen	十四	jū yon
15 fifteen	十五	jū go

| 16 sixteen | 十六 | jū roku |
| 17 seventeen | 十七 | jū shichi |

18 eighteen	十八	jū hachi
19 nineteen	十九	jū kyū
20 twenty	二十	ni jū
30 thirty	三十	san jū
40 forty	四十	yon jū
50 fifty	五十	go jū
60 sixty	六十	roku jū
70 seventy	七十	nana jū
80 eighty	八十	hachi jū
90 ninety	九十	kyū jū
100 one hundred	百	hyaku
200 two hundred	二百	ni hyaku
300 three hundred	三百	san byaku
400 four hundred	四百	yon hyaku
500 five hundred	五百	go hyaku
600 six hundred	六百	roppyaku
700 seven hundred	七百	nana hyaku
800 eight hundred	八百	happyaku
900 nine hundred	九百	kyū hyaku
1000 one thousand	千	sen
10000 ten thousand	一万	ichiman
one hundred thousand	１０万	jyūman
million	百万	hyakuman
billion	十億	jūoku

3. Humans. Family

man (adult male)	男性	dansei
young man	若者	wakamono
teenager	ティーンエージャー	tīnējā
woman	女性	josei
girl (young woman)	少女	shōjo
age	年齢	nenrei
adult (adj)	大人	otona
middle-aged (adj)	中年の	chūnen no
elderly (adj)	年配の	nenpai no
old (adj)	老いた	oi ta
old man	老人	rōjin
old woman	老婦人	rō fujin
retirement	退職	taishoku
to retire (from job)	退職する	taishoku suru
retiree	退職者	taishoku sha

mother	母親	hahaoya
father	父親	chichioya
son	息子	musuko
daughter	娘	musume
brother	兄、弟、兄弟	ani, otōto, kyoōdai
elder brother	兄	ani
younger brother	弟	otōto
sister	姉、妹、姉妹	ane, imōto, shimai
elder sister	姉	ane
younger sister	妹	imōto
parents	親	oya
child	子供	kodomo
children	子供	kodomo
stepmother	継母	keibo
stepfather	継父	keifu
grandmother	祖母	sobo
grandfather	祖父	sofu
grandson	孫息子	mago musuko
granddaughter	孫娘	mago musume
grandchildren	孫	mago
uncle	伯父	oji
aunt	伯母	oba
nephew	甥	oi
niece	姪	mei
wife	妻	tsuma
husband	夫	otto
married (masc.)	既婚の	kikon no
married (fem.)	既婚の	kikon no
widow	未亡人	mibōjin
widower	男やもめ	otokoyamome
name (first name)	名前	namae
surname (last name)	姓	sei
relative	親戚	shinseki
friend (masc.)	友達	tomodachi
friendship	友情	yūjō
partner	パートナー	pātonā
superior (n)	上司、上役	jōshi, uwayaku
colleague	同僚	dōryō
neighbors	隣人	rinjin

4. Human body

organism (body)	人体	jintai
body	身体	shintai

heart	心臓	shinzō
blood	血液	ketsueki
brain	脳	nō
nerve	神経	shinkei

bone	骨	hone
skeleton	骸骨	gaikotsu
spine (backbone)	背骨	sebone
rib	肋骨	rokkotsu
skull	頭蓋骨	zugaikotsu

muscle	筋肉	kinniku
lungs	肺	hai
skin	肌	hada

head	頭	atama
face	顔	kao
nose	鼻	hana
forehead	額	hitai
cheek	頬	hō

mouth	口	kuchi
tongue	舌	shita
tooth	歯	ha
lips	唇	kuchibiru
chin	あご（頤）	ago

ear	耳	mimi
neck	首	kubi
throat	喉	nodo

eye	眼	me
pupil	瞳	hitomi
eyebrow	眉	mayu
eyelash	まつげ	matsuge

hair	髪の毛	kaminoke
hairstyle	髪形	kamigata
mustache	口ひげ	kuchihige
beard	あごひげ	agohige
to have (a beard, etc.)	生やしている	hayashi te iru
bald (adj)	はげ頭の	hageatama no

hand	手	te
arm	腕	ude
finger	指	yubi
nail	爪	tsume
palm	手のひら	tenohira

shoulder	肩	kata
leg	足 [脚]	ashi
foot	足	ashi

| knee | 膝 | hiza |
| heel | かかと ［踵］ | kakato |

back	背中	senaka
waist	腰	koshi
beauty mark	美人ぼくろ	bijinbokuro
birthmark (café au lait spot)	母斑	bohan

5. Medicine. Diseases. Drugs

health	健康	kenkō
well (not sick)	健康な	kenkō na
sickness	病気	byōki
to be sick	病気になる	byōki ni naru
ill, sick (adj)	病気の	byōki no

cold (illness)	風邪	kaze
to catch a cold	風邪をひく	kaze wo hiku
tonsillitis	狭心症	kyōshinshō
pneumonia	肺炎	haien
flu, influenza	インフルエンザ	infuruenza

runny nose (coryza)	鼻水	hanamizu
cough	咳	seki
to cough (vi)	咳をする	seki wo suru
to sneeze (vi)	くしゃみをする	kushami wo suru

stroke	脳卒中	nōsocchū
heart attack	心臓発作	shinzō hossa
allergy	アレルギー	arerugī
asthma	ぜんそく ［喘息］	zensoku
diabetes	糖尿病	tōnyō byō

tumor	腫瘍	shuyō
cancer	がん ［癌］	gan
alcoholism	アルコール依存症	arukōru izon shō
AIDS	エイズ	eizu
fever	発熱	hatsunetsu
seasickness	船酔い	fune yoi

bruise (hématome)	打ち身	uchimi
bump (lump)	たんこぶ	tankobu
to limp (vi)	足を引きずる	ashi wo hikizuru
dislocation	脱臼	dakkyū
to dislocate (vt)	脱臼する	dakkyū suru

fracture	骨折	kossetsu
burn (injury)	火傷	yakedo
injury	けが ［怪我］	kega

pain	痛み	itami
toothache	歯痛	shitsū
to sweat (perspire)	汗をかく	ase wo kaku
deaf (adj)	ろうの [聾の]	rō no
mute (adj)	口のきけない	kuchi no kike nai
immunity	免疫	meneki
virus	ウィルス	wirusu
microbe	細菌	saikin
bacterium	バクテリア	bakuteria
infection	伝染	densen
hospital	病院	byōin
cure	療養	ryōyō
to vaccinate (vt)	予防接種をする	yobō sesshu wo suru
to be in a coma	昏睡状態になる	konsui jōtai ni naru
intensive care	集中治療	shūchū chiryō
symptom	兆候	chōkō
pulse	脈拍	myakuhaku

6. Feelings. Emotions. Conversation

I, me	私	watashi
you	あなた	anata
he	彼	kare
she	彼女	kanojo
we	私たち	watashi tachi
you (to a group)	あなたがた	anata ga ta
they	彼らは	karera wa
Hello! (fam.)	やあ！	yā!
Hello! (form.)	こんにちは！	konnichiwa!
Good morning!	おはよう！	ohayō!
Good afternoon!	こんにちは！	konnichiwa!
Good evening!	こんばんは！	konbanwa!
to say hello	こんにちはと言う	konnichiwa to iu
to greet (vt)	挨拶する	aisatsu suru
How are you?	元気？	genki ?
How are you? (form.)	お元気ですか？	wo genki desu ka?
How are you? (fam.)	元気？	genki ?
Bye-Bye! Goodbye!	さようなら！	sayōnara!
Goodbye! (form.)	さようなら！	sayōnara!
Bye! (fam.)	バイバイ！	baibai!
Thank you!	ありがとう！	arigatō!
feelings	感情	kanjō
to be hungry	腹をすかす	hara wo sukasu

to be thirsty	喉が渇く	nodo ga kawaku
tired (adj)	疲れた	tsukare ta
to be worried	心配する	shinpai suru
to be nervous	緊張する	kinchō suru
hope	希望	kibō
to hope (vi, vt)	希望する	kibō suru
character	性格	seikaku
modest (adj)	謙遜な	kenson na
lazy (adj)	怠惰な	taida na
generous (adj)	気前のよい	kimae no yoi
talented (adj)	才能のある	sainō no aru
honest (adj)	正直な	shōjiki na
serious (adj)	真剣な	shinken na
shy, timid (adj)	内気な	uchiki na
sincere (adj)	心からの	kokorokara no
coward	臆病者	okubyō mono
to sleep (vi)	眠る	nemuru
dream	夢	yume
bed	ベッド、寝台	beddo, shindai
pillow	枕	makura
insomnia	不眠症	fuminshō
to go to bed	就寝する	shūshin suru
nightmare	悪夢	akumu
alarm clock	目覚まし時計	mezamashi dokei
smile	ほほえみ［微笑み］	hohoemi
to smile (vi)	ほほえむ［微笑む］	hohoemu
to laugh (vi)	笑う	warau
quarrel	口論	kōron
insult	侮辱	bujoku
resentment	恨み	urami
angry (mad)	怒って	okotte

7. Clothing. Personal accessories

clothes	洋服	yōfuku
coat (overcoat)	オーバーコート	ōbā kōto
fur coat	毛皮のコート	kegawa no kōto
jacket (e.g., leather ~)	ジャケット	jaketto
raincoat (trenchcoat, etc.)	レインコート	reinkōto
shirt (button shirt)	ワイシャツ	waishatsu
pants	ズボン	zubon
suit jacket	ジャケット	jaketto

suit	背広	sebiro
dress (frock)	ドレス	doresu
skirt	スカート	sukāto
T-shirt	Tシャツ	tīshatsu
bathrobe	バスローブ	basurōbu
pajamas	パジャマ	pajama
workwear	作業服	sagyō fuku
underwear	下着	shitagi
socks	靴下	kutsushita
bra	ブラジャー	burajā
pantyhose	パンティストッキング	pantī sutokkingu
stockings (thigh highs)	ストッキング	sutokkingu
bathing suit	水着	mizugi
hat	帽子	bōshi
footwear	靴	kutsu
boots (cowboy ~)	ブーツ	būtsu
heel	かかと [踵]	kakato
shoestring	靴ひも	kutsu himo
shoe polish	靴クリーム	kutsu kurīmu
cotton (n)	綿	men
wool (n)	羊毛	yōmō
fur (n)	毛皮	kegawa
gloves	手袋	tebukuro
mittens	ミトン	miton
scarf (muffler)	マフラー	mafurā
glasses (eyeglasses)	めがね [眼鏡]	megane
umbrella	傘	kasa
tie (necktie)	ネクタイ	nekutai
handkerchief	ハンカチ	hankachi
comb	くし [櫛]	kushi
hairbrush	ヘアブラシ	hea burashi
buckle	バックル	bakkuru
belt	ベルト	beruto
purse	ハンドバッグ	hando baggu
collar	襟	eri
pocket	ポケット	poketto
sleeve	袖	sode
fly (on trousers)	ズボンのファスナー	zubon no fasunā
zipper (fastener)	チャック	chakku
button	ボタン	botan
to get dirty (vi)	汚れる	yogoreru
stain (mark, spot)	染み	shimi

8. City. Urban institutions

store	店、…屋	mise, …ya
shopping mall	ショッピングモール	shoppingu mōru
supermarket	スーパーマーケット	sūpāmāketto
shoe store	靴屋	kutsuya
bookstore	本屋	honya

drugstore, pharmacy	薬局	yakkyoku
bakery	パン屋	panya
candy store	菓子店	kashi ten
grocery store	食料品店	shokuryō hin ten
butcher shop	肉屋	nikuya
produce store	八百屋	yaoya
market	市場	ichiba

hair salon	美容院	biyō in
post office	郵便局	yūbin kyoku
dry cleaners	クリーニング屋	kurīningu ya
circus	サーカス	sākasu
zoo	動物園	dōbutsu en

theater	劇場	gekijō
movie theater	映画館	eiga kan
museum	博物館	hakubutsukan
library	図書館	toshokan

mosque	モスク	mosuku
synagogue	シナゴーグ	shinagōgu
cathedral	大聖堂	dai seidō
temple	寺院	jīn
church	教会	kyōkai

college	大学	daigaku
university	大学	daigaku
school	学校	gakkō

hotel	ホテル	hoteru
bank	銀行	ginkō
embassy	大使館	taishikan
travel agency	旅行代理店	ryokō dairi ten

subway	地下鉄	chikatetsu
hospital	病院	byōin
gas station	ガソリンスタンド	gasorin sutando
parking lot	駐車場	chūsha jō

ENTRANCE	入口	iriguchi
EXIT	出口	deguchi
PUSH	押す	osu
PULL	引く	hiku

| OPEN | 営業中 | eigyō chū |
| CLOSED | 休業日 | kyūgyōbi |

monument	記念碑	kinen hi
fortress	要塞	yōsai
palace	宮殿	kyūden

medieval (adj)	中世の	chūsei no
ancient (adj)	古代の	kodai no
national (adj)	国の	kuni no
well-known (adj)	有名な	yūmei na

9. Money. Finances

money	お金	okane
coin	コイン	koin
dollar	ドル	doru
euro	ユーロ	yūro

ATM	ＡＴＭ	ētīemu
currency exchange	両替所	ryōgae sho
exchange rate	為替レート	kawase rēto
cash	現金	genkin

How much?	いくら？	ikura ?
to pay (vi, vt)	払う	harau
payment	支払い	shiharai
change (give the ~)	おつり	o tsuri

price	価格	kakaku
discount	割引	waribiki
cheap (adj)	安い	yasui
expensive (adj)	高い	takai

bank	銀行	ginkō
account	口座	kōza
credit card	クレジットカード	kurejitto kādo
check	小切手	kogitte
to write a check	小切手を書く	kogitte wo kaku
checkbook	小切手帳	kogitte chō

debt	債務	saimu
debtor	債務者	saimu sha
to lend (money)	貸す	kasu
to borrow (vi, vt)	借りる	kariru

to rent (~ a tuxedo)	レンタルする	rentaru suru
on credit (adv)	付けで	tsuke de
wallet	財布	saifu
safe	金庫	kinko

inheritance	相続	sōzoku
fortune (wealth)	財産	zaisan
tax	税	zei
fine	罰金	bakkin
to fine (vt)	罰金を科す	bakkin wo kasu
wholesale (adj)	卸売の	oroshiuri no
retail (adj)	小売の	kōri no
to insure (vt)	保険をかける	hoken wo kakeru
insurance	保険	hoken
capital	資本	shihon
turnover	売上高	uriage daka
stock (share)	株	kabu
profit	利益	rieki
profitable (adj)	利益のある	rieki no aru
crisis	危機	kiki
bankruptcy	破産	hasan
to go bankrupt	破産する	hasan suru
accountant	会計士	kaikeishi
salary	給料	kyūryō
bonus (money)	ボーナス	bōnasu

10. Transportation

bus	バス	basu
streetcar	路面電車	romen densha
trolley bus	トロリーバス	tororībasu
to go by ...	…で行く	… de iku
to get on (~ the bus)	乗る	noru
to get off ...	降りる	oriru
stop (e.g., bus ~)	停	toma
terminus	終着駅	shūchakueki
schedule	時刻表	jikoku hyō
ticket	乗車券	jōsha ken
to be late (for ...)	遅れる	okureru
taxi, cab	タクシー	takushī
by taxi	タクシーで	takushī de
taxi stand	タクシー乗り場	takushī noriba
traffic	交通	kōtsū
rush hour	ラッシュアワー	rasshuawā
to park (vi)	駐車する	chūsha suru
subway	地下鉄	chikatetsu

station	駅	eki
train	列車	ressha
train station	鉄道駅	tetsudō eki
rails	レール	rēru
compartment	コンパートメント	konpātomento
berth	寝台	shindai

airplane	航空機	kōkūki
air ticket	航空券	kōkū ken
airline	航空会社	kōkū gaisha
airport	空港	kūkō

flight (act of flying)	飛行	hikō
luggage	荷物	nimotsu
luggage cart	荷物カート	nimotsu kāto

ship	船舶	senpaku
cruise ship	遠洋定期船	enyō teiki sen
yacht	ヨット	yotto
boat (flat-bottomed ~)	ボート	bōto

captain	船長	senchō
cabin	船室	senshitsu
port (harbor)	港	minato

bicycle	自転車	jitensha
scooter	スクーター	sukūtā
motorcycle, bike	オートバイ	ōtobai
pedal	ペダル	pedaru
pump	ポンプ	ponpu
wheel	車輪	sharin

automobile, car	自動車	jidōsha
ambulance	救急車	kyūkyū sha
truck	トラック	torakku
used (adj)	中古の	chūko no
car crash	車の事故	kuruma no jiko
repair	修理	shūri

11. Food. Part 1

meat	肉	niku
chicken	鶏	niwatori
duck	ダック	dakku
pork	豚肉	buta niku
veal	子牛肉	kōshi niku
lamb	子羊肉	kohitsuji niku
beef	牛肉	gyū niku
sausage (bologna, pepperoni, etc.)	ソーセージ	sōsēji

egg	卵	tamago
fish	魚	sakana
cheese	チーズ	chīzu
sugar	砂糖	satō
salt	塩	shio

rice	米	kome
pasta	パスタ	pasuta
butter	バター	batā
vegetable oil	植物油	shokubutsu yu
bread	パン	pan
chocolate (n)	チョコレート	chokorēto

wine	ワイン	wain
coffee	コーヒー	kōhī
milk	乳、ミルク	nyū, miruku
juice	ジュース	jūsu

| beer | ビール | bīru |
| tea | 茶 | cha |

tomato	トマト	tomato
cucumber	きゅうり［胡瓜］	kyūri
carrot	ニンジン［人参］	ninjin
potato	ジャガイモ	jagaimo

| onion | たまねぎ［玉葱］ | tamanegi |
| garlic | ニンニク | ninniku |

cabbage	キャベツ	kyabetsu
beetroot	テーブルビート	tēburu bīto
eggplant	ナス	nasu
dill	ディル	diru

| lettuce | レタス | retasu |
| corn (maize) | トウモロコシ | tōmorokoshi |

fruit	果物	kudamono
apple	リンゴ	ringo
pear	洋梨	yōnashi
lemon	レモン	remon

| orange | オレンジ | orenji |
| strawberry | イチゴ（苺） | ichigo |

plum	プラム	puramu
raspberry	ラズベリー（木苺）	razuberī
pineapple	パイナップル	painappuru
banana	バナナ	banana
watermelon	スイカ	suika
grape	ブドウ［葡萄］	budō
melon	メロン	meron

12. Food. Part 2

cuisine	料理	ryōri
recipe	レシピ	reshipi
food	食べ物	tabemono
to have breakfast	朝食をとる	chōshoku wo toru
to have lunch	昼食をとる	chūshoku wo toru
to have dinner	夕食をとる	yūshoku wo toru
taste, flavor	味	aji
tasty (adj)	美味しい	oishī
cold (adj)	冷たい	tsumetai
hot (adj)	熱い	atsui
sweet (sugary)	甘い	amai
salty (adj)	塩味の	shioaji no
sandwich (bread)	サンドイッチ	sandoicchi
side dish	付け合わせ	tsukeawase
filling (for cake, pie)	フィリング	firingu
sauce	ソース	sōsu
piece (of cake, pie)	一切れ	ichi kire
diet	ダイエット	daietto
vitamin	ビタミン	bitamin
calorie	カロリー	karorī
vegetarian (n)	ベジタリアン	bejitarian
restaurant	レストラン	resutoran
coffee house	喫茶店	kissaten
appetite	食欲	shokuyoku
Enjoy your meal!	どうぞお召し上がり下さい！	dōzo o meshiagarikudasai!
waiter	ウェイター	weitā
waitress	ウェートレス	wētoresu
bartender	バーテンダー	bātendā
menu	メニュー	menyū
spoon	スプーン	supūn
knife	ナイフ	naifu
fork	フォーク	fōku
cup (e.g., coffee ~)	カップ	kappu
plate (dinner ~)	皿	sara
saucer	ソーサー	sōsā
napkin (on table)	ナフキン	nafukin
toothpick	つまようじ［爪楊枝］	tsumayōji
to order (meal)	注文する	chūmon suru
course, dish	料理	ryōri

portion	一人前	ichi ninmae
appetizer	前菜	zensai
salad	サラダ	sarada
soup	スープ	sūpu
dessert	デザート	dezāto
whole fruit jam	ジャム	jamu
ice-cream	アイスクリーム	aisukurīmu
check	お勘定	okanjō
to pay the check	勘定を払う	kanjō wo harau
tip	チップ	chippu

13. House. Apartment. Part 1

house	家屋	kaoku
country house	田舎の邸宅	inaka no teitaku
villa (seaside ~)	別荘	bessō
floor, story	階	kai
entrance	入口	iriguchi
wall	壁	kabe
roof	屋根	yane
chimney	煙突	entotsu
attic (storage place)	屋根裏	yaneura
window	窓	mado
window ledge	窓台	mado dai
balcony	バルコニー	barukonī
stairs (stairway)	階段	kaidan
mailbox	郵便受け	yūbin uke
garbage can	ゴミ収納庫	gomishūnōko
elevator	エレベーター	erebētā
electricity	電気	denki
light bulb	電球	denkyū
switch	スイッチ	suicchi
wall socket	コンセント	konsento
fuse	ヒューズ	hyūzu
door	ドア	doa
handle, doorknob	ドアノブ	doa nobu
key	鍵	kagi
doormat	玄関マット	genkan matto
door lock	錠	jō
doorbell	ドアベル	doa beru
knock (at the door)	ノック	nokku
to knock (vi)	ノックする	nokku suru

peephole	ドアアイ	doaai
yard	中庭	nakaniwa
garden	庭	niwa
swimming pool	プール	pūru
gym (home gym)	ジム	jimu
tennis court	テニスコート	tenisu kōto
garage	車庫	shako

private property	私有地	shiyūchi
warning sign	警告表示	keikoku hyōji
security	警備	keibi
security guard	警備員	keibi in

renovations	リフォーム	rifōmu
to renovate (vt)	リフォームする	rifōmu suru
to put in order	整頓する	seiton suru
to paint (~ a wall)	塗る	nuru
wallpaper	壁紙	kabegami
to varnish (vt)	ニスを塗る	nisu wo nuru

pipe	管	kan
tools	工具	kōgu
basement	地下室	chika shitsu
sewerage (system)	下水道	gesuidō

14. House. Apartment. Part 2

apartment	アパート	apāto
room	部屋	heya
bedroom	寝室	shinshitsu
dining room	食堂	shokudō

living room	居間	ima
study (home office)	書斎	shosai
entry room	玄関	genkan
bathroom (room with a bath or shower)	浴室	yokushitsu
half bath	トイレ	toire

| floor | 床 | yuka |
| ceiling | 天井 | tenjō |

to dust (vt)	ほこりを払う	hokori wo harau
vacuum cleaner	掃除機	sōji ki
to vacuum (vt)	掃除機をかける	sōji ki wo kakeru

mop	モップ	moppu
dust cloth	ダストクロス	dasuto kurosu
short broom	ほうき	hōki
dustpan	ちりとり	chiritori

furniture	家具	kagu
table	テーブル	tēburu
chair	椅子	isu
armchair	肘掛け椅子	hijikake isu

bookcase	書棚	shodana
shelf	棚	tana
wardrobe	ワードローブ	wādo rōbu

mirror	鏡	kagami
carpet	カーペット	kāpetto
fireplace	暖炉	danro
drapes	カーテン	kāten
table lamp	テーブルランプ	tēburu ranpu
chandelier	シャンデリア	shanderia

kitchen	台所	daidokoro
gas stove (range)	ガスコンロ	gasu konro
electric stove	電気コンロ	denki konro
microwave oven	電子レンジ	denshi renji

refrigerator	冷蔵庫	reizōko
freezer	冷凍庫	reitōko
dishwasher	食器洗い機	shokkiarai ki
faucet	蛇口	jaguchi

meat grinder	肉挽き器	niku hiki ki
juicer	ジューサー	jūsā
toaster	トースター	tōsutā
mixer	ハンドミキサー	hando mikisā

coffee machine	コーヒーメーカー	kōhī mēkā
kettle	やかん	yakan
teapot	急須	kyūsu

TV set	テレビ	terebi
VCR (video recorder)	ビデオ	bideo
iron (e.g., steam ~)	アイロン	airon
telephone	電話	denwa

15. Professions. Social status

director	責任者	sekinin sha
superior	上司	jōshi
president	社長	shachō
assistant	助手	joshu
secretary	秘書	hisho

| owner, proprietor | 経営者 | keieisha |
| partner | パートナー | pātonā |

stockholder	株主	kabunushi
businessman	ビジネスマン	bijinesuman
millionaire	百万長者	hyakuman chōja
billionaire	億万長者	okuman chōja
actor	俳優	haiyū
architect	建築士	kenchiku shi
banker	銀行家	ginkō ka
broker	仲買人	nakagainin
veterinarian	獣医	jūi
doctor	医者	isha
chambermaid	客室係	kyakushitsu gakari
designer	デザイナー	dezainā
correspondent	特派員	tokuhain
delivery man	宅配業者	takuhai gyōsha
electrician	電気工事士	denki kōji shi
musician	音楽家	ongakuka
babysitter	ベビーシッター	bebīshittā
hairdresser	美容師	biyō shi
herder, shepherd	牛飼い	ushikai
singer (masc.)	歌手	kashu
translator	翻訳者	honyaku sha
writer	作家	sakka
carpenter	大工	daiku
cook	料理人	ryōri jin
fireman	消防士	shōbō shi
police officer	警官	keikan
mailman	郵便配達人	yūbin haitatsu jin
programmer	プログラマー	puroguramā
salesman (store staff)	店員	tenin
worker	労働者	rōdō sha
gardener	庭師	niwashi
plumber	配管工	haikan kō
dentist	歯科医	shikai
flight attendant (fem.)	客室乗務員	kyakushitsu jōmu in
dancer (masc.)	ダンサー	dansā
bodyguard	ボディーガード	bodīgādo
scientist	科学者	kagaku sha
schoolteacher	教師	kyōshi
farmer	農業経営者	nōgyō keiei sha
surgeon	外科医	gekai
miner	鉱山労働者	kōzan rōdō sha
chef (kitchen chef)	シェフ	shefu
driver	運転手	unten shu

16. Sport

kind of sports	スポーツの種類	supōtsu no shurui
soccer	サッカー	sakkā
hockey	アイスホッケー	aisuhokkē
basketball	バスケットボール	basukettobōru
baseball	野球	yakyū
volleyball	バレーボール	barēbōru
boxing	ボクシング	bokushingu
wrestling	レスリング	resuringu
tennis	テニス	tenisu
swimming	水泳	suiei
chess	チェス	chesu
running	ランニング	ranningu
athletics	陸上競技	rikujō kyōgi
figure skating	フィギュアスケート	figyua sukēto
cycling	サイクリング	saikuringu
billiards	ビリヤード	biriyādo
bodybuilding	ボディビル	bodibiru
golf	ゴルフ	gorufu
scuba diving	ダイビング	daibingu
sailing	セーリング	sēringu
archery	洋弓	yōkyū
period, half	ピリオド、ハーフ	piriodo, hāfu
half-time	ハーフタイム	hāfu taimu
tie	引き分け	hikiwake
to tie (vi)	引き分けになる	hikiwake ni naru
treadmill	トレッドミル	toreddomiru
player	選手	senshu
substitute	補欠	hoketsu
substitutes bench	ベンチ	benchi
match	試合	shiai
goal	ゴール	gōru
goalkeeper	ゴールキーパー	gōrukīpā
goal (score)	ゴール	gōru
Olympic Games	オリンピック	orinpikku
to set a record	記録を打ち立てる	kiroku wo uchitateru
final	決勝戦	kesshō sen
champion	チャンピオン	chanpion
championship	選手権	senshuken
winner	勝利者	shōri sha
victory	勝利	shōri
to win (vi)	勝つ	katsu

to lose (not win)	負ける	makeru
medal	メダル	medaru
first place	一位	ichi i
second place	二位	ni i
third place	三位	san i
stadium	スタジアム	sutajiamu
fan, supporter	ファン	fan
trainer, coach	トレーナー	torēnā
training	トレーニング	torēningu

17. Foreign languages. Orthography

language	言語	gengo
to study (vt)	勉強する	benkyō suru
pronunciation	発音	hatsuon
accent	なまり [訛り]	namari
noun	名詞	meishi
adjective	形容詞	keiyōshi
verb	動詞	dōshi
adverb	副詞	fukushi
pronoun	代名詞	daimeishi
interjection	間投詞	kantōshi
preposition	前置詞	zenchishi
root	語根	gokon
ending	語尾	gobi
prefix	接頭辞	settō ji
syllable	音節	onsetsu
suffix	接尾辞	setsubi ji
stress mark	キョウセイ [強勢]	kyōsei
period, dot	句点	kuten
comma	コンマ	konma
colon	コロン	koron
ellipsis	省略	shōrya ku
question	疑問文	gimon bun
question mark	疑問符	gimon fu
exclamation point	感嘆符	kantan fu
in quotation marks	引用符内	inyō fu nai
in parenthesis	ガッコ内 （括弧内）	kakko nai
letter	文字	moji
capital letter	大文字	daimonji
sentence	文	bun
group of words	語群	gogun

expression	表現	hyōgen
subject	主語	shugo
predicate	述語	jutsugo
line	行	gyō
paragraph	段落	danraku

synonym	同義語	dōgigo
antonym	対義語	taigigo
exception	例外	reigai
to underline (vt)	下線を引く	kasen wo hiku

rules	規則	kisoku
grammar	文法	bunpō
vocabulary	語彙	goi
phonetics	音声学	onseigaku
alphabet	アルファベット	arufabetto

textbook	教科書	kyōkasho
dictionary	辞書	jisho
phrasebook	慣用表現集	kanyō hyōgen shū

word	単語	tango
meaning	意味	imi
memory	記憶	kioku

18. The Earth. Geography

the Earth	地球	chikyū
the globe (the Earth)	世界	sekai
planet	惑星	wakusei

geography	地理学	chiri gaku
nature	自然	shizen
map	地図	chizu
atlas	地図帳	chizu chō

in the north	北に	kita ni
in the south	南に	minami ni
in the west	西に	nishi ni
in the east	東に	higashi ni

sea	海	umi
ocean	海洋	kaiyō
gulf (bay)	湾	wan
straits	海峡	kaikyō

continent (mainland)	大陸	tairiku
island	島	shima
peninsula	半島	hantō
archipelago	多島海	tatōkai

harbor	泊地	hakuchi
coral reef	サンゴ礁	sangoshō
shore	海岸	kaigan
coast	沿岸	engan
flow (flood tide)	満潮	manchō
ebb (ebb tide)	干潮	kanchō
latitude	緯度	ido
longitude	経度	keido
parallel	度線	dosen
equator	赤道	sekidō
sky	空	sora
horizon	地平線	chiheisen
atmosphere	大気	taiki
mountain	山	yama
summit, top	頂上	chōjō
cliff	断崖	dangai
hill	丘	oka
volcano	火山	kazan
glacier	氷河	hyōga
waterfall	滝	taki
plain	平原	heigen
river	川	kawa
spring (natural source)	泉	izumi
bank (of river)	川岸	kawagishi
downstream (adv)	下流の	karyū no
upstream (adv)	上流の	jōryū no
lake	湖	mizūmi
dam	ダム	damu
canal	運河	unga
swamp (marshland)	沼地	numachi
ice	氷	kōri

19. Countries of the world. Part 1

Europe	ヨーロッパ	yōroppa
European Union	欧州連合	ōshū rengō
European (n)	ヨーロッパ人	yōroppa jin
European (adj)	ヨーロッパの	yōroppa no
Austria	オーストリア	ōsutoria
Great Britain	グレートブリテン島	gurētoburiten tō
England	イギリス	igirisu
Belgium	ベルギー	berugī

Germany	ドイツ	doitsu
Netherlands	ネーデルラント	nēderuranto
Holland	オランダ	oranda
Greece	ギリシャ	girisha
Denmark	デンマーク	denmāku
Ireland	アイルランド	airurando
Iceland	アイスランド	aisurando
Spain	スペイン	supein
Italy	イタリア	itaria
Cyprus	キプロス	kipurosu
Malta	マルタ	maruta
Norway	ノルウェー	noruwē
Portugal	ポルトガル	porutogaru
Finland	フィンランド	finrando
France	フランス	furansu
Sweden	スウェーデン	suwēden
Switzerland	スイス	suisu
Scotland	スコットランド	sukottorando
Vatican	バチカン	bachikan
Liechtenstein	リヒテンシュタイン	rihitenshutain
Luxembourg	ルクセンブルク	rukusenburuku
Monaco	モナコ	monako
Albania	アルバニア	arubania
Bulgaria	ブルガリア	burugaria
Hungary	ハンガリー	hangarī
Latvia	ラトビア	ratobia
Lithuania	リトアニア	ritoania
Poland	ポーランド	pōrando
Romania	ルーマニア	rūmania
Serbia	セルビア	serubia
Slovakia	スロバキア	surobakia
Croatia	クロアチア	kuroachia
Czech Republic	チェコ	cheko
Estonia	エストニア	esutonia
Bosnia and Herzegovina	ボスニア・ ヘルツェゴヴィナ	bosunia herutsegovina
Macedonia (Republic of ~)	マケドニア地方	makedonia chihō
Slovenia	スロベニア	surobenia
Montenegro	モンテネグロ	monteneguro
Belarus	ベラルーシー	berarūshī
Moldova, Moldavia	モルドヴァ	morudova
Russia	ロシア	roshia
Ukraine	ウクライナ	ukuraina

20. Countries of the world. Part 2

Asia	アジア	ajia
Vietnam	ベトナム	betonamu
India	インド	indo
Israel	イスラエル	isuraeru
China	中国	chūgoku
Lebanon	レバノン	rebanon
Mongolia	モンゴル	mongoru
Malaysia	マレーシア	marēshia
Pakistan	パキスタン	pakisutan
Saudi Arabia	サウジアラビア	saujiarabia
Thailand	タイ	tai
Taiwan	台湾	taiwan
Turkey	トルコ	toruko
Japan	日本	nihon
Afghanistan	アフガニスタン	afuganisutan
Bangladesh	バングラデシュ	banguradeshu
Indonesia	インドネシア	indoneshia
Jordan	ヨルダン	yorudan
Iraq	イラク	iraku
Iran	イラン	iran
Cambodia	カンボジア	kanbojia
Kuwait	クウェート	kuwēto
Laos	ラオス	raosu
Myanmar	ミャンマー	myanmā
Nepal	ネパール	nepāru
United Arab Emirates	アラブ首長国連邦	arabu shuchō koku renpō
Syria	シリア	shiria
Palestine	パレスチナ	paresuchina
South Korea	大韓民国	daikanminkoku
North Korea	北朝鮮	kitachōsen
United States of America	アメリカ合衆国	amerika gasshūkoku
Canada	カナダ	kanada
Mexico	メキシコ	mekishiko
Argentina	アルゼンチン	aruzenchin
Brazil	ブラジル	burajiru
Colombia	コロンビア	koronbia
Cuba	キューバ	kyūba
Chile	チリ	chiri
Venezuela	ベネズエラ	benezuera
Ecuador	エクアドル	ekuadoru
The Bahamas	バハマ	bahama
Panama	パナマ	panama

Egypt	エジプト	ejiputo
Morocco	モロッコ	morokko
Tunisia	チュニジア	chunijia
Kenya	ケニア	kenia
Libya	リビア	ribia
South Africa	南アフリカ	minami afurika
Australia	オーストラリア	ōsutoraria
New Zealand	ニュージーランド	nyūjīrando

21. Weather. Natural disasters

weather	天気	tenki
weather forecast	天気予報	tenki yohō
temperature	温度	ondo
thermometer	温度計	ondo kei
barometer	気圧計	kiatsu kei
sun	太陽	taiyō
to shine (vi)	照る	teru
sunny (day)	晴れの	hare no
to come up (vi)	昇る	noboru
to set (vi)	沈む	shizumu
rain	雨	ame
it's raining	雨が降っている	ame ga futte iru
pouring rain	土砂降りの雨	doshaburi no ame
rain cloud	雨雲	amagumo
puddle	水溜り	mizutamari
to get wet (in rain)	ぬれる [濡れる]	nureru
thunderstorm	雷雨	raiu
lightning (~ strike)	稲妻	inazuma
to flash (vi)	ピカッと光る	pikatto hikaru
thunder	雷	kaminari
it's thundering	雷が鳴っている	kaminari ga natte iru
hail	ひょう [雹]	hyō
it's hailing	ひょうが降っている	hyō ga futte iru
heat (extreme ~)	猛暑	mōsho
it's hot	暑いです	atsui desu
it's warm	暖かいです	atatakai desu
it's cold	寒いです	samui desu
fog (mist)	霧	kiri
foggy	霧の	kiri no
cloud	雲	kumo
cloudy (adj)	曇りの	kumori no
humidity	湿度	shitsudo
snow	雪	yuki

it's snowing	雪が降っている	yuki ga futte iru
frost (severe ~, freezing cold)	ひどい霜	hidoi shimo
below zero (adv)	零下	reika
hoarfrost	霜	shimo
bad weather	悪い天気	warui tenki
disaster	災害	saigai
flood, inundation	洪水	kōzui
avalanche	雪崩	nadare
earthquake	地震	jishin
tremor, quake	震動	shindō
epicenter	震源地	shingen chi
eruption	噴火	funka
lava	溶岩	yōgan
tornado	竜巻	tatsumaki
twister	旋風	senpū
hurricane	ハリケーン	harikēn
tsunami	津波	tsunami
cyclone	サイクロン	saikuron

22. Animals. Part 1

animal	動物	dōbutsu
predator	肉食獣	nikushoku juu
tiger	トラ [虎]	tora
lion	ライオン	raion
wolf	オオカミ	ōkami
fox	キツネ [狐]	kitsune
jaguar	ジャガー	jagā
lynx	オオヤマネコ	ōyamaneko
coyote	コヨーテ	koyōte
jackal	ジャッカル	jakkaru
hyena	ハイエナ	haiena
squirrel	リス	risu
hedgehog	ハリネズミ [針鼠]	harinezumi
rabbit	ウサギ [兎]	usagi
raccoon	アライグマ	araiguma
hamster	ハムスター	hamusutā
mole	モグラ	mogura
mouse	ネズミ	nezumi
rat	ラット	ratto
bat	コウモリ [蝙蝠]	kōmori
beaver	ビーバー	bībā

horse	ウマ［馬］	uma
deer	シカ［鹿］	shika
camel	ラクダ［駱駝］	rakuda
zebra	シマウマ［縞馬］	shimauma
whale	クジラ［鯨］	kujira
seal	アザラシ	azarashi
walrus	セイウチ［海象］	seiuchi
dolphin	いるか［海豚］	iruka
bear	クマ［熊］	kuma
monkey	サル［猿］	saru
elephant	ゾウ［象］	zō
rhinoceros	サイ［犀］	sai
giraffe	キリン	kirin
hippopotamus	カバ［河馬］	kaba
kangaroo	カンガルー	kangarū
cat	猫	neko
dog	犬	inu
cow	雌牛	meushi
bull	雄牛	ōshi
sheep (ewe)	羊	hitsuji
goat	ヤギ［山羊］	yagi
donkey	ロバ	roba
pig, hog	ブタ［豚］	buta
hen (chicken)	ニワトリ［鶏］	niwatori
rooster	おんどり［雄鶏］	ondori
duck	アヒル	ahiru
goose	ガチョウ	gachō
turkey (hen)	七面鳥［シチメンチョウ］	shichimenchō
sheepdog	牧羊犬	bokuyō ken

23. Animals. Part 2

bird	鳥	tori
pigeon	鳩［ハト］	hato
sparrow	スズメ（雀）	suzume
tit	シジュウカラ［四十雀］	shijūkara
magpie	カササギ（鵲）	kasasagi
eagle	鷲	washi
hawk	鷹	taka
falcon	ハヤブサ［隼］	hayabusa
swan	白鳥［ハクチョウ］	hakuchō
crane	鶴［ツル］	tsuru
stork	シュバシコウ	shubashikō

parrot	オウム	ōmu
peacock	クジャク [孔雀]	kujaku
ostrich	ダチョウ [駝鳥]	dachō
heron	サギ [鷺]	sagi
nightingale	サヨナキドリ	sayonakidori
swallow	ツバメ [燕]	tsubame
woodpecker	キツツキ	kitsutsuki
cuckoo	カッコウ [郭公]	kakkō
owl	トラフズク	torafuzuku
penguin	ペンギン	pengin
tuna	マグロ [鮪]	maguro
trout	マス [鱒]	masu
eel	ウナギ [鰻]	unagi
shark	サメ [鮫]	same
crab	カニ [蟹]	kani
jellyfish	クラゲ [水母]	kurage
octopus	タコ [蛸]	tako
starfish	ヒトデ [海星]	hitode
sea urchin	ウニ [海胆]	uni
seahorse	タツノオトシゴ	tatsunootoshigo
shrimp	エビ	ebi
snake	ヘビ (蛇)	hebi
viper	クサリヘビ	kusarihebi
lizard	トカゲ [蜥蜴]	tokage
iguana	イグアナ	iguana
chameleon	カメレオン	kamereon
scorpion	サソリ [蠍]	sasori
turtle	カメ [亀]	kame
frog	蛙 [カエル]	kaeru
crocodile	ワニ [鰐]	wani
insect, bug	昆虫	konchū
butterfly	チョウ [蝶]	chō
ant	アリ [蟻]	ari
fly	ハエ [蠅]	hae
mosquito	カ [蚊]	ka
beetle	甲虫	kabutomushi
bee	ハチ [蜂]	hachi
spider	クモ [蜘蛛]	kumo

24. Trees. Plants

tree	木	ki
birch	カバノキ	kabanoki

oak	オーク	ōku
linden tree	シナノキ [科の木]	shinanoki
aspen	ヤマナラシ [山鳴らし]	yamanarashi

maple	カエデ [楓]	kaede
spruce	スプルース	supurūsu
pine	マツ [松]	matsu
cedar	シダー	shidā

poplar	ポプラ	popura
rowan	ナナカマド	nanakamado
beech	ブナ	buna
elm	ニレ [楡]	nire

ash (tree)	トネリコ [梣]	toneriko
chestnut	クリ [栗]	kuri
palm tree	ヤシ [椰子]	yashi
bush	低木	teiboku

mushroom	キノコ [茸]	kinoko
poisonous mushroom	毒キノコ	doku kinoko
cep (Boletus edulis)	ヤマドリタケ	yamadori take
russula	ベニタケ [紅茸]	beni take
fly agaric	ベニテングタケ [紅天狗茸]	benitengu take
death cap	タマゴテングタケ [卵天狗茸]	tamagotengu take

flower	花	hana
bouquet (of flowers)	花束	hanataba
rose (flower)	バラ	bara
tulip	チューリップ	chūrippu
carnation	カーネーション	kānēshon

camomile	カモミール	kamomīru
cactus	サボテン	saboten
lily of the valley	スズラン [鈴蘭]	suzuran
snowdrop	スノードロップ	sunōdoroppu
water lily	スイレン [睡蓮]	suiren

greenhouse (tropical ~)	温室	onshitsu
lawn	芝生	shibafu
flowerbed	花壇	kadan

plant	植物	shokubutsu
grass	草	kusa
leaf	葉	ha
petal	花びら	hanabira
stem	茎	kuki
young plant (shoot)	シュート	shūto
cereal crops	禾穀類	kakokurui
wheat	コムギ [小麦]	komugi

rye	ライムギ [ライ麦]	raimugi
oats	オーツムギ [オーツ麦]	ōtsu mugi
millet	キビ [黍]	kibi
barley	オオムギ [大麦]	ōmugi
corn	トウモロコシ	tōmorokoshi
rice	イネ [稲]	ine

25. Various useful words

balance (of situation)	衡平	kōhei
base (basis)	基礎	kiso
beginning	始め	hajime
category	カテゴリー	kategorī
choice	選択	sentaku
coincidence	一致	icchi
comparison	比較	hikaku
degree (extent, amount)	程度	teido
development	発達	hattatsu
difference	差異	sai
effect (e.g., of drugs)	効果	kōka
effort (exertion)	尽力	jinryoku
element	要素	yōso
example (illustration)	例	rei
fact	事実	jijitsu
help	手伝い	tetsudai
ideal	理想	risō
kind (sort, type)	種類	shurui
mistake, error	間違い	machigai
moment	瞬間	shunkan
obstacle	妨害	bōgai
part (~ of sth)	一部	ichibu
pause (break)	一時停止	ichiji teishi
position	位置	ichi
problem	問題	mondai
process	一連の作業	ichiren no sagyō
progress	進歩	shinpo
property (quality)	性質	seishitsu
reaction	反応	hannō
risk	危険	kiken
secret	秘密	himitsu
series	シリーズ	shirīzu

shape (outer form)	形状	keijō
situation	状況	jōkyō
solution	解決	kaiketsu
standard (adj)	標準の	hyōjun no

stop (pause)	休止	kyūshi
style	スタイル	sutairu
system	システム	shisutemu
table (chart)	表	hyō
tempo, rate	テンポ	tenpo

term (word, expression)	用語	yōgo
truth (e.g., moment of ~)	真実	shinjitsu
turn (please wait your ~)	順番	junban
urgent (adj)	至急の	shikyū no

utility (usefulness)	実用性	jitsuyō sei
variant (alternative)	バリアント	barianto
way (means, method)	方法	hōhō
zone	地帯	chitai

26. Modifiers. Adjectives. Part 1

additional (adj)	追加の	tsuika no
ancient (~ civilization)	古代の	kodai no
artificial (adj)	人工の	jinkō no
bad (adj)	悪い	warui
beautiful (person)	美しい	utsukushī

big (in size)	大きい	ohkī
bitter (taste)	苦い	nigai
blind (sightless)	盲目の	mōmoku no
central (adj)	中心の	chūshin no

children's (adj)	子供の	kodomo no
clandestine (secret)	内密の	naimitsu no
clean (free from dirt)	きれいな	kireina
clever (smart)	利口な	rikō na
compatible (adj)	…準拠の	… junkyo no

contented (satisfied)	満足した	manzoku shi ta
dangerous (adj)	危険な	kiken na
dead (not alive)	死んだ	shin da
dense (fog, smoke)	濃い	koi
difficult (decision)	難しい	muzukashī

dirty (not clean)	汚れた	yogore ta
easy (not difficult)	易しい	yasashī
empty (glass, room)	空の	karano
exact (amount)	正確な	seikaku na

excellent (adj)	優れた	sugure ta
excessive (adj)	過度の	kado no
exterior (adj)	外部の	gaibu no
fast (quick)	速い	hayai
fertile (land, soil)	肥えた	koe ta
fragile (china, glass)	壊れやすい	koware yasui
free (at no cost)	無料の	muryō no
fresh (~ water)	淡…	tan …
frozen (food)	冷凍の	reitō no
full (completely filled)	満ちた	michi ta
happy (adj)	幸福な	kōfuku na
hard (not soft)	硬い	katai
huge (adj)	巨大な	kyodai na
ill (sick, unwell)	病気の	byōki no
immobile (adj)	動けない	ugoke nai
important (adj)	重要な	jūyō na
interior (adj)	内部の	naibu no
last (e.g., ~ week)	先…	sen …
last (final)	最後の	saigo no
left (e.g., ~ side)	左の	hidari no
legal (legitimate)	合法の	gōhō no
light (in weight)	軽い	karui
liquid (fluid)	液状の	ekijō no
long (e.g., ~ hair)	長い	nagai
loud (voice, etc.)	大声の	ōgoe no
low (voice)	低い	hikui

27. Modifiers. Adjectives. Part 2

main (principal)	主な	omo na
matt, matte	マット	matto
mysterious (adj)	謎の	nazo no
narrow (street, etc.)	狭い	semai
native (~ country)	生まれた	umare ta
negative (~ response)	否定の	hitei no
new (adj)	新しい	atarashī
next (e.g., ~ week)	来…	rai …
normal (adj)	標準の	hyōjun no
not difficult (adj)	難しくない	muzukashiku nai
obligatory (adj)	義務的な	gimu teki na
old (house)	古い	furui
open (adj)	開いた	hirai ta
opposite (adj)	正反対の	sei hantai no
ordinary (usual)	普通の	futsū no

original (unusual)	独創的な	dokusōtekina
personal (adj)	個人的な	kojin teki na
polite (adj)	礼儀正しい	reigi tadashī
poor (not rich)	貧乏な	binbō na
possible (adj)	可能な	kanō na
principal (main)	主な	omo na
probable (adj)	ありそうな	arisō na
prolonged (e.g., ~ applause)	連続的な	renzoku teki na
public (open to all)	公共の	kōkyō no
rare (adj)	珍しい	mezurashī
raw (uncooked)	生の	nama no
right (not left)	右の	migi no
ripe (fruit)	熟れた	ure ta
risky (adj)	危険な	kiken na
sad (~ look)	悲しげな	kanashi ge na
second hand (adj)	中古の	chūko no
shallow (water)	浅い	asai
sharp (blade, etc.)	鋭い	surudoi
short (in length)	短い	mijikai
similar (adj)	に似て	ni ni te
small (in size)	小さい	chīsai
smooth (surface)	平坦な	heitan na
soft (~ toys)	柔らかい	yawarakai
solid (~ wall)	頑丈な	ganjō na
sour (flavor, taste)	酸っぱい [すっぱい]	suppai
spacious (house, etc.)	広々とした	hirobiro to shi ta
special (adj)	特別の	tokubetsu no
straight (line, road)	直…、真っすぐな	choku …, massuguna
strong (person)	強い	tsuyoi
stupid (foolish)	愚かな	oroka na
superb, perfect (adj)	優れた	sugure ta
sweet (sugary)	甘い	amai
tan (adj)	日焼けした	hiyake shi ta
tasty (delicious)	美味しい	oishī
unclear (adj)	明確でない	meikaku de nai

28. Verbs. Part 1

to accuse (vt)	責める	semeru
to agree (say yes)	同意する	dōi suru
to announce (vt)	アナウンスする	anaunsu suru
to answer (vi, vt)	回答する	kaitō suru

to apologize (vi)	謝る	ayamaru
to arrive (vi)	到着する	tōchaku suru
to ask (~ oneself)	問う	tō
to be absent	欠席する	kesseki suru
to be afraid	怖がる	kowagaru
to be born	生まれる	umareru
to be in a hurry	急ぐ	isogu
to beat (to hit)	殴る	naguru
to begin (vt)	始める	hajimeru
to believe (in God)	信じる	shinjiru
to belong to …	所有物である	shoyū butsu de aru
to break (split into pieces)	折る、壊す	oru, kowasu
to build (vt)	建設する	kensetsu suru
to buy (purchase)	買う	kau
can (v aux)	できる	dekiru
can (v aux)	できる	dekiru
to cancel (call off)	取り消す	torikesu
to catch (vt)	捕らえる	toraeru
to change (vt)	変える	kaeru
to check (to examine)	検査する	kensa suru
to choose (select)	選択する	sentaku suru
to clean up (tidy)	掃除をする	sōji wo suru
to close (vt)	閉める	shimeru
to compare (vt)	比較する	hikaku suru
to complain (vi, vt)	不平を言う	fuhei wo iu
to confirm (vt)	確認する	kakunin suru
to congratulate (vt)	祝う	iwau
to cook (dinner)	料理をする	ryōri wo suru
to copy (vt)	コピーする	kopī suru
to cost (vt)	かかる	kakaru
to count (add up)	計算する	keisan suru
to count on …	…を頼りにする	… wo tayori ni suru
to create (vt)	創造する	sōzō suru
to cry (weep)	泣く	naku
to dance (vi, vt)	踊る	odoru
to deceive (vi, vt)	だます	damasu
to decide (~ to do sth)	決定する	kettei suru
to delete (vt)	削除する	sakujo suru
to demand (request firmly)	要求する	yōkyū suru
to deny (vt)	否定する	hitei suru
to depend on …	…に依存する	… ni izon suru
to despise (vt)	軽蔑する	keibetsu suru
to die (vi)	死ぬ	shinu
to dig (vt)	掘る	horu

to disappear (vi)	姿を消す	sugata wo kesu
to discuss (vt)	討議する	tōgi suru
to disturb (vt)	邪魔をする	jama wo suru

29. Verbs. Part 2

to dive (vi)	ダイビングする	daibingu suru
to divorce (vi)	離婚する	rikon suru
to do (vt)	する	suru
to doubt (have doubts)	疑う	utagau
to drink (vi, vt)	飲む	nomu
to drop (let fall)	落とす	otosu
to dry (clothes, hair)	乾かす	kawakasu
to eat (vi, vt)	食べる	taberu
to end (~ a relationship)	終わらせる	owaraseru
to excuse (forgive)	許す	yurusu
to exist (vi)	存在する	sonzai suru
to expect (foresee)	見越す	mikosu
to explain (vt)	説明する	setsumei suru
to fall (vi)	落ちる	ochiru
to fight (street fight, etc.)	喧嘩をする	kenka wo suru
to find (vt)	見つける	mitsukeru
to finish (vt)	終える	oeru
to fly (vi)	飛ぶ	tobu
to forbid (vt)	禁じる	kinjiru
to forget (vi, vt)	忘れる	wasureru
to forgive (vt)	許す	yurusu
to get tired	疲れる	tsukareru
to give (vt)	手渡す	tewatasu
to go (on foot)	行く	iku
to hate (vt)	憎む	nikumu
to have (vt)	持つ	motsu
to have breakfast	朝食をとる	chōshoku wo toru
to have dinner	夕食をとる	yūshoku wo toru
to have lunch	昼食をとる	chūshoku wo toru
to hear (vt)	聞く	kiku
to help (vt)	手伝う	tetsudau
to hide (vt)	隠す	kakusu
to hope (vi, vt)	希望する	kibō suru
to hunt (vi, vt)	狩る	karu
to hurry (vi)	急ぐ	isogu
to insist (vi, vt)	主張する	shuchō suru
to insult (vt)	侮辱する	bujoku suru

to invite (vt)	招待する	shōtai suru
to joke (vi)	冗談を言う	jōdan wo iu
to keep (vt)	保つ	tamotsu

to kill (vt)	殺す	korosu
to know (sb)	知っている	shitte iru
to know (sth)	知る	shiru
to like (I like ...)	好む	konomu
to look at ...	…を見る	… wo miru

to lose (umbrella, etc.)	なくす	nakusu
to love (sb)	愛する	aisuru
to make a mistake	誤りをする	ayamari wo suru
to meet (vi, vt)	会う	au
to miss (school, etc.)	欠席する	kesseki suru

30. Verbs. Part 3

to obey (vi, vt)	従う	shitagau
to open (vt)	開ける	akeru
to participate (vi)	参加する	sanka suru
to pay (vi, vt)	払う	harau
to permit (vt)	許可する	kyoka suru

to play (children)	遊ぶ	asobu
to pray (vi, vt)	祈る	inoru
to promise (vt)	約束する	yakusoku suru
to propose (vt)	提案する	teian suru
to prove (vt)	証明する	shōmei suru
to read (vi, vt)	読む	yomu

to receive (vt)	受け取る	uketoru
to rent (sth from sb)	借りる	kariru
to repeat (say again)	復唱する	fukushō suru
to reserve, to book	予約する	yoyaku suru
to run (vi)	走る	hashiru

to save (rescue)	救出する	kyūshutsu suru
to say (~ thank you)	言う	iu
to see (vt)	見る	miru
to sell (vt)	売る	uru
to send (vt)	送る	okuru
to shoot (vi)	撃つ	utsu

to shout (vi)	叫ぶ	sakebu
to show (vt)	見せる	miseru
to sign (document)	署名する	shomei suru
to sing (vi)	さえずる	saezuru
to sit down (vi)	座る	suwaru
to smile (vi)	ほほえむ［微笑む］	hohoemu

to speak (vi, vt)	話す	hanasu
to steal (money, etc.)	盗む	nusumu
to stop (please ~ calling me)	止める	tomeru
to study (vt)	勉強する	benkyō suru

to swim (vi)	泳ぐ	oyogu
to take (vt)	取る	toru
to talk to …	…と話す	… to hanasu
to tell (story, joke)	話をする	hanashi wo suru
to thank (vt)	感謝する	kansha suru
to think (vi, vt)	思う	omō

to translate (vt)	翻訳する	honyaku suru
to trust (vt)	信用する	shinyō suru
to try (attempt)	試みる	kokoromiru
to turn (e.g., ~ left)	曲がる	magaru
to turn off	消す	kesu

to turn on	つける	tsukeru
to understand (vt)	理解する	rikai suru
to wait (vt)	待つ	matsu
to want (wish, desire)	欲する	hossuru
to work (vi)	働く	hataraku
to write (vt)	書く	kaku